Contents

CREATIVE CAREERS

W11960

370·11

FACTORY

This book is due for return on or before the last date shown below.

-8 FEB 2005
0 3 NOV 2022

trotman

To Mum and Dad

Editorial and Publishing Team
Author Tania Shillam
Editorial Mina Patria, Editorial Director; Rachel Lockhart, Commissioning
Editor; Anya Wilson, Editor; Erin Milliken, Editorial Assistant
Production Ken Ruskin, Head of Pre-press and Production
Sales and Marketing Deborah Jones, Head of Sales and Marketing
Managing Director Toby Trotman

Designed by XAB

British Library Cataloguing in Publication Data
A catalogue record for this book is available from the British Library

ISBN 0 85660 902 1

Typeset by Mac Style Ltd, Scarborough, N. Yorkshire
Printed and bound in Great Britain by The Cromwell Press,
Trowbridge, Wiltshire

About the author

CBS INC., World Headquarters
51 West 52nd Street, New York
1995

The building known as 'Blackrock' housed executives and the major broadcast talent for the CBS radio and television networks. Blackrock was known for high security and exclusive access so when this very well dressed businesswoman with closely shorn hair resembling Sinead O'Connor somehow made it past my assistant's desk and appeared at my office door I simply remarked, 'Nice hair'. Her succinct and extremely British reply was 'I was told by CBS Radio Networks Programming that we should chat'. This was the first time Tania and I met.

The years in which it has taken Ms Shillam to compile the information in this book have been based on a focused initiative and desire to achieve, learn and pass along that knowledge. The qualities she used to procure and establish the initial meetings with the country's top executives and talent has since been employed to cultivate a close circle of friends on both sides of the Atlantic.

Tania brought that same energy to Washington DC recently to broadcast with me on my morning show via the global Worldspace Satellite Radio Network and XM in the United States.

Remember as you read on:

Believe in your own **talent**.
Access the information and thoughts contained in this book.
Build and reinforce your **network** of contacts.
Always have the confidence to take the **initiative** in your life.
These steps could very well allow the **access** to realise your dreams.

TED KELLY
DIRECTOR, GLOBAL MEDIA MARKETING AND
PROMOTION, WORLDSPACE SATELLITE RADIO
PROGRAM DIRECTOR / MORNING PRESENTER - UPOP
WORLDSPACE/XM2

Acknowledgements

There are gems to be found in these pages from people in the industry who contributed time and effort and generous spirit to this book. With humility and gratitude I would like to acknowledge: James Healy of Chelsea & Westminster Hospital Radio; Des Shepherd of Broadcast Training Ltd; Aimee Lake at Sony; Sarah Lowther from Bloomberg Radio; Ola French from BBC LDN 94.9; Roger Harrabin from BBC Radio 4's 'Today' programme; Andy Brown from BBC Radio 1 and 1Xtra; Henry Bonsu from BBC LDN 94.9; Mark Simpson from BBC Radio 2; Neil Gardner of Ladbroke Productions (Radio) Ltd; Steve Ackerman of Somethin' Else; Julia Chapman of NCI Management Ltd; Mike Chapman of Spydaradio; and John Taylor of Fiction Factory for closing my book with his literary flourish and, finally, Owen Bennett Jones, my first radio teacher.

Trotman would like to thank Adam Gee, James Estill, Julian Mobbs and Katie Streten at Channel 4's **IDEAS**FACTORY for their editorial input and guidance.

'Radio can take the listener into worlds they never expected to come across.'

so you want to work in radio?

By the time you finish this book I want you to be imagining your acceptance speech at the Sony Awards. The Sonys are the radio version of the Oscars. They award producers, broadcasters, programmes and stations for putting art, creativity and undivided passion into radio. These are the people who can put gems into their programmes and jewels into your ears.

Start dreaming the dream now! Here are some examples of the beauty of radio as recognised by the Sony judges. See if you relate to any of them: 'The History of Funk' by the production company Somethin' Else; Radio 5's news programme, 'Up All Night'; Radio 4's comedy programme 'Goodness Gracious Me'; Radio 4's 'Today'; Jonathan Ross's Saturday morning show on Radio 2 and Christian O'Connell's breakfast programme on Xfm. There is an endless variety of the type of programme and subject matter that they award.

Radio can take the listener into worlds they never expected to come across, into a subject they thought they had no interest in, into topics they had no knowledge of. Even when broadcasting terrible news, a turn of phrase, good choice of vocabulary, clear articulation of an idea and imaginative selection of interviewee will have a lasting impression on the listener.

Those with a passion for radio will tell you that it is the highest form of broadcasting. Some people use radio as a stepping-stone into a TV career. If that is your motivation then there is no reason to be any less passionate about the quality of your research, the creativity in your ideas, the way in which you go about informing yourself and the enthusiasm with which you approach the programme content. Experience in radio will stand you in good stead for working on any topic in any media.

SO YOU WANT TO WORK IN RADIO?

Why does your future lie in radio? You've got to stand out above thousands of others. Write down your answer and keep refining it as you make your way through this book. You might find the task daunting and difficult to start with, but as time goes on and fine-tuning takes place, this could end up being your description of yourself on your CV. There's a section on CV writing in Chapter 8.

Who do you admire on the radio? Is this person in music radio or speech radio? Is it their voice and delivery you like or their subject? Do you want to be a producer or a presenter? Do you want to have your own production company? (Did you know that there are companies that exist only to supply stations with 'content'?) Would you like to be a reporter on a travel programme or the Middle East expert for a news organisation?

WHAT THIS BOOK WILL DO FOR YOU

To get into radio you will need to set your goal, focus your energy and proceed armed with knowledge and confidence. This book will show you what the industry wants from you. There's no two ways about it – they want a lot! This book will tell you about the attitude radio expects its newcomers to have. There are interviews from people who point the way forward.

Facts and figures

Ninety-one per cent of adults listen to the radio every day. The average listening time is 3.5 hours according to the 2003 *Guardian Media Guide*, edited by Steve Peak. It's no wonder that politicians, celebrities and publicity seekers parade relentlessly through radio studios, one after the other.

There are writing examples and exercises for you to do. There are tips on how to train yourself and how to get into good habits. There are contacts to help you find entry points to the industry and there are plenty of opportunities (suggested websites and books) for you to put in your own research.

You can't just sit down and read this book. As you work through the pages, make use of the advice and tick off the suggestions and tasks. By the time you finally present yourself on the doorstep of the radio industry you'll have armed yourself with enough self-reliance and information to make an impressive entry.

IMMERSE YOURSELF IN RADIO AT HOME

Listen broadly and have an idea of the styles of many stations. Think about your listening habits and, whatever they are, broaden them! Invest in a radio that allows you to flick through the channels easily.

What presenters do you listen to? How do you think your hero or heroine got into their job? If you don't know, find out. How did they get enough knowledge of their field to be a credible presenter? How did they acquire the qualifications and experience? What path did the programme director of a station or the chief executive of a small production company take?

Look it up on the internet, get down to the library, read their profiles in magazines. Make it a project to get the answers to these questions. You *must* know what you're up against and be clear and confident about what you have to offer.

If you only listen to pirate radio, we need to talk! Did you want to spend your whole career riding the turntables for the Street Massive! Yes, you know they are illegal set-ups and I know that some are very community spirited and play music not carried on major radio stations. Some have led to brilliant legitimate careers for a number of presenters. The pirate

The most popular station is Radio 2 with 12.9 million listeners. The most popular commercial radio station is Classic FM with just over half that figure. Radio 1 comes in with 10.5 million listeners (*2003 Guardian Media Guide*). In a country with a population of only 60 million that's an incredible hold over the adult population.

There are 310 radio stations: 50 are part of the BBC and the rest are commercial. Imagine how many radio jobs are out there!

phenomenon also, eventually, goes legitimate and some radio stations that exist today have a proud pirate history. We could argue about this subject all the way through the book.

However, if you want a career in radio you will have to start listening to radio that is **structured**, that is presented by professionals with an **extensive vocabulary** and the ability to **articulate** and be **widely understood**. As a student of radio you will need access to equipment that you won't find in a pirate station. Try retuning while you're making your way though this book. We need to give your ears a real workout! Pirate radio follows fashions which, by their nature, change. Whether the underground music of the moment is pop, punk, garage or hip hop, whether the icons of the moment are the elegant Mod-style suited boys or desperate Britney-style prostitute-chic girls, you will need skills, skills and more skills.

One thing you don't need is a criminal record. If you're convicted of working in a pirate station you cannot work in broadcasting *in any capacity* for five years.

TYPES OF RADIO AND FORMATS

There's BBC national and local radio and there's the commercial sector. There's digital, cable, satellite and Internet. On the smaller and more interesting level, as far as getting into a radio career is concerned, there's community and access radio, student and hospital radio and 'RSL' (see Chapter 2) or festival radio, and don't forget in-store radio. All of these types of radio are programmed in a variety of formats. Whichever format you work in, you will be applying the same skills and standards. All formats come under two general terms: Speech radio and Music radio – each covering a huge variety of different genres and audiences.

SPEECH RADIO

News
Is this for you? There are many, many news radio stations, news programmes and independent news providers for radio. Almost every station has news bulletins scattered throughout the schedule. You may want to read the news on your favourite station, or you may want to be a foreign correspondent for the BBC World Service. What about heading up a newsroom ladder to be the editor of a major news programme or even run a news provider service?

This is a very tough, relentlessly active and demanding career and incredibly rewarding. You'll have to be on red alert all the time for information, updates, contacts, breaking stories and different perspectives, and you'll be expected to have a 'nose for news'. Don't be surprised if employers ask for a degree and a couple of languages at the more demanding end of the scale. There are a lot of training courses tailored to the news journalist. You won't be lost for entry points.

Sport

Do you have a medal box overflowing with your running, cycling, swimming and cricketing achievements? Do you stop everything for the tennis and the Tour de France? If you live for sport but didn't make the Olympic grade you can make a career out of following the ones who do. For this career you may well need journalist training. When, for example, football riots break out, you'll have to cover events as a news journalist would. You have to be familiar with the main sports: football, cricket, rugby, basketball and ice hockey. Sport programming is not as sexist as people think – there are as many women presenting sports programmes as men. Where are the entry points? I know of a GCSE student who volunteered at the local football grounds and, on the strength of that, got work experience at a local paper reporting on the matches. Any employer at a radio station would love such enthusiasm and dedication.

Talk

Do you like phone-in programmes, interactive radio and studio discussions? Do you like to hear what ordinary, unscripted people have to say? When Talk Radio began in 1995 many callers said that it was as if democracy was sweeping the country. It seems a very quaint idea now but at the time it felt very powerful and a break from the tight world of contrived political opinions flooding the radio airwaves. Anything could be discussed, from the steady decline of the Conservative Party, through gun control, to 'how does it feel to find your husband in bed with another man'!

In 1995 the idea of the 'shock jock' was scandalising the moral certainties of the country and the radio world. Caesar the Geezer was doing most of the scandalising. The idea came from the USA in the shock jock days of the OJ Simpson's trial and transformed itself into a British radio phenomenon with a British flavour. Today the format is widely adopted and phone-in programmes really do give radio a sense of democracy. This kind of radio will give a wonderful career to a meticulous producer or a quick-witted and articulate presenter. As an entry point, a job as a phone op will

give you a spectacular vantage point to see
how programmes work and what callers are
actually like.

Drama

Do you listen to plays, readings, poetry and
short stories on the radio? Do you want to
write original plays for radio or create
adaptations of books or dramatisations of
novels? There are so many opportunities to
hear this kind of broadcasting on BBC Radio 4
and Radio 5 and now there is a digital station,
One Word, which is wall-to-wall book-based
radio. You'll be someone who loves language
and characters and plot. A job as a production
assistant will provide a great learning curve.
If you have secretarial skills you'll be ahead
of a lot of the competition.

Magazine programmes

These are for people who want to be up-to-
date on a variety of subjects. They cover
whatever is of contemporary interest. It might
be a topical book, a newsworthy personality, a
sporting event, an event in history or a
current burning issue. It will have regular
features and irregular guests. It will be studio based and have outside
broadcasts and use pre-records and live discussions. It's exactly like
turning the pages of a magazine; you'll find a lively mixture.

MUSIC RADIO

Music radio represents a large proportion of radio output. Here's a career
that will indulge your music tastes and keep your CD collection constantly
updated. If music is your way of life and you have galaxies of knowledge to
offer then you'll love a radio career. You'll be doing your research at gigs
and concerts. You'll be mixing with creative people and you'll be the first to
know of the latest trends and scenes. At BBC 1Xtra you might be the latest
talent to be spotted and feted. At a commercial radio station you may be
working on the top 40, organising interviews with the top artists. At a
classical radio station you may be making programmes about modern

mini-Mozarts or the history of percussion. There are opportunities for every kind of person in music radio. You don't have to be the hedonistic type. For entry points try out your skills in a local hospital radio, community radio, university radio station or with work experience at a local station. There are many opportunities to cut your teeth in this field. A Restricted Service Licence (RSL) would be a good place to start (see Chapter 2, page 10).

From music radio to hard-hitting factual programmes, the production needs of different styles of radio can be, of course, entirely different but there are some common themes. Wherever you work you'll have to be aware of the **target audience** and their interests. In all areas of radio you'll need to **write well** and with confidence and you must always have **ideas** to offer.

Once you get used to the terms used in the industry there'll be few surprises as you move around from station to station or programme to programme. There is a certain language adopted by the industry. You'll get used to hearing about booking guests, running orders, scripts, interview notes, and packages.

On my first day at BBC Radio 1 I was told that my job as a production assistant would include 'packing boxes'. I was flabbergasted: I wasn't there to be any kind of removal man! I had visions of offices that had to be rearranged and of huge cardboard boxes. The office was a chaotic mess; each desk was an island of mess. Well, let me allay any fears. The box referred to is the black box that a presenter takes into the studio which is full of CDs to be played (packed in order), script ready to follow, any competition details and prizes, headphones, and anything else the presenter may need – perhaps a book if the author is due in as a guest. It is the job of the production assistant to 'pack the box'!

WHAT ARE THE JOBS?

Let's have a look at the major jobs in radio. All of these descriptions vary according to what area you work in. A newsroom will make different demands to a drama department, for example. Many workplaces expect flexibility from their workforce, titles change, and many programmes are presenter-only shows. The descriptions are hopefully broad enough to cover the type of job you can expect. The more local the radio, the more you'll be expected to cover lots of roles. Get used to looking at the *Media Guardian* on Mondays and Saturdays and the descriptions given in the job adverts.

A **Radio Production Assistant** will co-ordinate and book people and studios, type scripts and check details, put things into order and do paperwork. Not to mention sending out competition prizes and answering the phone and responding to letters and emails. This is the busy-bee job in radio. It's an excellent place to get to know the ropes.

A **Broadcast Assistant** will support the producer and presenter. There will be admin to do as well as research and production. There are lots of similarities with the Production Assistant role. What you are called might depend on whether you're working in the BBC, commercial sector, national or local. It's potentially an all-round job where you can get production and technical skills.

A **Producer** can stamp his or her personality on the programme. This will be done by initiating ideas, coming up with new features and revamping the old ones. In a large team this is a planning and creative job. If a programme consists of only a presenter and a producer then all the legwork, detail and technicalities are taken care of by the producer. A producer will also take care of the programme's budget and represent the programme at station editorial meetings. Tight deadlines are a producer's noose.

Technical operator/studio producer. There's an interview later in the book with a techie. Whatever sound you hear, whether generated in a studio or on location, it is down to the studio operator who manages all the technical aspects of making live radio possible. In pre-recorded radio this is the person who can record, edit and mix the audio.

Find out what the job requirements are for a **Presenter**, a **Broadcast Journalist** and a **Researcher**. Take a look at the Prospects Planner website (www.prospects.ac.uk/links/occupations) which gives immensely detailed occupational profiles including salary ranges, possible entry requirements and career progression. Make sure you also check out the **IDEAS**FACTORY careers section, for information about different job roles and how to get in: www.ideasfactory.com/careers/index.htm. Another good source of information about job roles is the Skillsformedia site: go to www.skillsformedia.com, click on 'What's inside' and follow the links for careers advice.

'Nothing stands in the way of your getting started and getting broadcast!'

you can be at the heart of radio making

GCSEs OR VOCATIONAL TRAINING?

It honestly doesn't matter what subject you choose. You must concern yourself with getting a broad education. Always attend to your general knowledge and take pride in gathering skills, information and interests. Don't only think of what you study at school or college but also the hobbies you do in your free time. Is it sport or playing an instrument? Do you represent the county at something? Do you write for a publication? Whatever you do, do it well.

Many people will tell you that competition is too fierce to proceed without a good standard of education. To counter that argument there are many, many broadcasters and producers without a hint of a formal qualification. Why not leave school at 16, some say, and start from the bottom? In the five years you might have spent getting A-levels and going to university you'll know everything there is to know about radio. You'll have settled into your career by the time the graduate comes along and has to start from the beginning. It's a good argument.

However, every possible survey suggests that, on average, graduates earn much more than non-graduates. If you study something other than media then you may have prepared for an alternative profession if the radio option falls through. A university education gives you an area of expertise, discipline and years of constant writing practice. You'll come away with the ability to distil ideas, philosophies and arguments down to their essence, whether you study politics or civil engineering. You'll be a whiz at pulling different arguments together into a structured thesis.

I took Politics and American Studies and so spent a year studying in New York. My brother and sister included languages in their degree options and so spent their years abroad in France. You cannot dismiss such opportunities lightly. The cost of a degree is, of course, a huge political issue and a hard personal decision for many but if, in the future, you want to spend three years (possibly abroad) studying and working in the local radio station, how much do you think that will cost and how much of a headache to organise? Think of all those wonderful subjects that are there for you to savour. What lights your fire? Go and study it!

GRASS ROOTS RADIO

Here's some very exciting information: nothing stands in the way of your getting started and getting broadcast! Not the lack of a degree, not the lack of a BBC training course, not the lack of work experience, not the lack of a staff job in a station! You can get into radio through a Restricted Service Licence (RSL).

This is how the Radio Authority website describes RSLs:

Low powered radio licences for a particular establishment or other defined location or particular event. These embrace long-term hospital and student services and short-term 'trials', i.e. ahead of possible permanent licences to test and/or demonstrate demand and 'special event' stations.

What this really means is that you can be at the heart of radio making in no time. If your area is having a carnival or festival, it is possible that a community group of some description has applied for and been granted a licence. They are going to need your help. Take a look at the Radio Authority website (www.radioauthority.org.uk) where you can find an up-to-date list of current licences together with the reason for the station and contact details. There is also a list of future allocations of a broadcast frequency. Here are some examples:

- Avenues FM in London for youth project/training
- Corby Radio to raise awareness of a fund-raising project in the community
- Crescent Radio in Rochdale to celebrate the birth of the Holy Prophet Muhammad
- European Tour Radio in Virginia Water for the Golf Championship
- Forest FM in Verwood incorporating Verwood Carnival celebrations
- Harborough FM in Market Harborough to promote the carnival.

And so the list goes on. Think of the interviews and packages (I'll explain what that is later) you could produce about Market Harborough, the Holy Prophet Muhammad, golf and everything else that's going on around the festival in the wider community. The broadcast radius of the station might be three to five miles – an intimate area. And that little world can be your oyster for 28 days.

Another way to find what RSLs are currently on air is to look at the UK Radio website (http://ukradio.com/). It calls itself 'the radio industry's most referenced news source'. It collects its news from radio stations and production houses all over the country. It's a source of news about very, very small, local radio concerns as well as news of radio at a national level.

HOSPITAL RADIO
The Radio Authority quote mentions 'hospital services'. Here's another world waiting to be your oyster. Some hospital services spread their remit beyond the boundaries of the hospital walls and are very active in the community. Some hospitals have a very active volunteer structure within the hospital to organise concerts and events for the patients. This will be reflected on their radio station.

James Healy: Station Manager of Chelsea & Westminster Hospital Radio in London.

Here is a good example of a hospital with an active volunteer network and a lot going on. It has an award-winning arts project that regularly organises recitals, choral works, world music and even entire operas. There are rich opportunities for variety in their programmes. Here's what James has to say about his experience of donating his time there.

How long have you worked at C&W?

James: I have worked at Radio Chelsea and Westminster since I was 20 so I have been there for the last five years. I have been Station Manager for the last year.

What made you volunteer?

James: I was interested in getting into broadcasting and it is *the* way to get into radio. It provides you with studio skills and, more importantly, it's a place where you can make your mistakes.

Is it all about requests and playing music?

James: Music represents the majority of our output, but we do have a news review programme on Saturday mornings. We have a schedule which has to reflect the varied tastes of the listeners. We also broadcast live concerts that take place in the hospital, so listeners who are unable to leave their beds can still enjoy the many events held at the hospital. We play classical music throughout the night. We have an impressive 24-hour music log which enables us to broadcast even when there is nobody in the studio.

Is there a recruitment procedure and what are you looking for?

James: Our station has a recruitment procedure and we're over-subscribed by people wanting to join. We receive unsolicited calls or emails from prospective volunteers which allows us to recruit roughly ten new members every three to six months.

Recruitment involves an interview by me and a probation period of usually a month or so. I'm looking for commitment and enthusiasm for the job. These are the prerequisites and this will remain valid if they progress further in broadcasting. The key part of the job is realising that you're an essential part of the hospital community.

What does a new recruit do? Is there training?

James: We do provide full training but it's important that we establish the volunteer's commitment to the job before we do so. New recruits start on one of our daily request shows. These take place every evening at 8.00 and it's our most interactive show as listeners are encouraged to call with their requests. Also, the new recruit will visit the wards to speak directly to patients.

Training is offered after six to nine months and includes all aspects of driving the desk. This means cuing tracks, playing jingles/sweepers/liners, voice work and learning basic presentation skills.

How much time does a new recruit need to give?

James: Commitment is massively important and even though the time given is fairly minimal (about two or three hours a week on a particular night), it's essential that the members turn up on a regular basis.

Any burning advice to give?

James: What we offer is a blank canvas and it's the perfect environment to cut your teeth in broadcasting. Of equal importance, the hospital community brings huge rewards through meeting patients, and realising that everybody has a story to tell is incredibly gratifying. After all, the pictures are always better on radio.

Nuneaton hospital radio started with enthusiasts and their dream, nothing more. In 1979, the council made available premises for a tiny rent and Philips provided the studio and distribution equipment at 'the right price'. Volunteers and enthusiasts launched a public appeal for funds and worked day and night to renovate the premises and build studios. After presenters were recruited and trained Anker Radio made its first broadcast on 6 November 1980.

Take a look at the website (www.geh.nhs.uk/anker/index1.htm) if you are in the area. There may be an appeal for volunteers. Otherwise, look up the hospital in your area and see what they offer and if they want you.

Anker Radio provides an astonishing story of people who adore radio enough to start a radio station from scratch. Any opportunity to mix with such enthusiasts should be taken without hesitation. Also, Anker gives a very high-tech description of its two broadcast studios, its jingles system and its seamless broadcasting. What a place to start your radio education!

Take a look at the Hospital Broadcasting Association website (www.hbauk.com/). It gives information about the National Hospital Radio Awards. Award categories include, as you would expect, station of the year, male and female broadcaster of the year and, sponsored by IRN (Independent Radio News) no less, speech package of the year. Imagine putting an IRN award on your CV!

Before you take yourself off to your local hospital radio do some research. Look it up. Look at others and make a comparison. Take a look at the website for Kingston Hospital Radio, for example. It's very detailed.

Here's another possibility. If you read through the history page of Anker Radio you'll see how crucial fundraising was to the dream project. You could offer your time and energy to a hospital radio as a fundraiser and see how a radio operation works from another angle.

Work in radio sales regularly makes the jobs pages. Fundraising is a skill that will look good on your CV. Take a look through the jobs pages and see how many charities and organisations need fundraisers. Do a search for radio sales jobs. It's an alternative and it can't hurt to have a few of those. It might provide you with an entry point into commercial radio in the future.

COMMUNITY RADIO

The Community Media Association (www.commedia.org.uk/back.htm) began life in 1983 as a broad coalition of campaigners and academics, unlicensed stations, radio production workshops and community activists. Its ethos is to acknowledge the growing community radio sector and reject private commercial gain. It exists to give information and training.

This means that new, very local, radio stations have access to legitimate broadcasting and the Association is working towards more and more devolution of the radio industry. For you, this means that opportunities to work in radio don't depend on the biggest broadcasters in the biggest cities producing the usual subjects and chasing the typical guests. Look at the website to see if there's a community station in your area.

Here is an example of an active community station. The Sound Vision Trust website is the very detailed website for Sound Radio (www.svt.org.uk/). This is how it describes itself:

> Since the start SVT has been involved in the heart of the community with projects ranging from music production courses through to Internet radio webcasts. Working both locally and internationally SVT is steadily fulfilling its aims of being a leading provider of skills, information and facilities to those who need them.

Its website gives news and training advice, and the schedule shows a wide variety of shows and music programmes from Latin American to Kurdish. There's also an appeal for volunteers.

STUDENT RADIO

If you go to university it's likely that you'll find a student radio station there. There are approximately 80 student radio groups across the country. It's a perfect opportunity to get hands-on experience in a part of the industry that favours cutting-edge music programming.

Student stations use a number of different broadcasting techniques: an RSL licence; an LPAM licence which means that the station broadcasts full time on AM, but is restricted to the campus; an Induction Loop which uses the AM frequency, and normally broadcasts only to a specific hall of residence or campus; a hard-wire system which broadcasts at specific times over a PA system to halls of residence or union buildings; and, finally, Internet broadcasting, which has a very wide reach.

Take a look at www.studentradio.org.uk to find out about them. The website is also a rich resource of fact sheets (including 'Essential guide for presenters', 'What makes bad radio?' 'Getting Started' and 'News for Student Radio'). There's a list of university radio stations and you can click to listen (www.studentradio.org.uk/station.php).

The Student Radio Association (SRA) is affiliated to the Radio Academy (RA) which is worth becoming a member of whether you're at university or not because of the access you'll get to training, information and advice. You'll find a link to its website via the SRA.

In-store radio

Take a look at these:

All:sports live from all:sports stores
Alldays Radio from Alldays stores
ASDAfm at ASDA supermarkets
BP Radio at BP garages
Costcutter Digital Radio in Costcutter stores
Homebase FM from Homebase stores
McCollsFM in McColls stores

Moto in Moto service stations
Nisa FM at Nisa Today's stores
Peninsula Radio in Pool Market, Cornwall
Tiles FM of Topps Tiles Clearance Centres
Tiles FM in Topps Tiles retail stores
VMR in Virgin Megastores record shops

See if you can find out about them, what they broadcast, whether they need volunteers or staff, whether they offer training and what kind of equipment they use. Find the contact details. Find out if they broadcast anywhere near you. See if you can find out what presenters or people in the industry cut their teeth on Homebase FM or mastered their trade at VMR.

GETTING STARTED

You don't have to wait for school to organise a work placement for you. Try your luck, if you feel confident enough, and organise it yourself. If you are decades past your GCSEs and reading this book as someone who wants a career change, this applies to you too. Call up and organise it yourself.

You could call your local radio station and ask to speak to the producer of a programme you like, or simply ask the receptionist who you should speak to. Ask who would be most amenable to the idea of having a volunteer on their programme. Call up your local hospital radio and offer a commitment of one evening a week. See if there's an RSL in your area.

Plan what you're going to say. Be **clear and articulate**, always. **Inspire confidence** in the person you're speaking to.

See if you can do a regular work experience shift (perhaps once a week) on a particular programme. They may prefer if you just do one dedicated 9-to-5 week. Whatever it is, you can help a producer by making teas and coffees, running errands, 'phone-bashing' and welcoming guests.

If that sounds boring then bear in mind that you'll be watching a producer and presenter at work, you'll be listening to interviews and studio discussions more closely than you would be at home and you'll become familiar with a programme style (music, magazine, news, phone-in) and station or 'in-house' style.

You'll see at first hand what kind of information and back-up the presenter needs from the producer. You'll see how a running order is used. You'll see if scripts are used or not and what research has been done. You'll see how a producer watches the clock and judges the length of interviews or the balance of phone contributions to studio discussion, or the amount of speech between tracks. My work experience was on the Bob Mills show on BBC GLR (coffee, white, with two sugars).

Be warned, though, you may find that you're put to no use at all in your stay with the station and that nobody takes very much interest. If you are still at school ask a teacher to help you on how to present yourself in the workplace, how to put yourself forward to take responsibilities for tasks, how to be keen and interested and perhaps pushy, even if it appears that your colleagues are not taking much notice of you. If you don't have access to a teacher, you might know someone in the industry, so ask for his or her advice. If not, sign up for a short course and ask the tutor for tips on how to impress. It's entirely down to you to inspire your colleagues to be interested in you.

There are tasks that are the standard, daily tasks. Find out what they are and offer to do them. Phone-bashing is always required. Arranging taxis for regular guests might be necessary. There are any number of ways in which you can make yourself useful. Also, if anyone offers to spend time with you, whether to show you equipment or go through a script or help you with a CV, *take them up on the offer.*

You should find an acceptable phone voice – this is the one you use for professional purposes and not the voice and language you use with your friends. If you think you need help in this then there are courses in public speaking where you will learn clear articulation and good use of language.

Don't ever sit in the corner of a studio with a glazed look and hunched-over posture. Have a notebook and always make notes of names (the people you're working with and the people being interviewed), subjects covered, reactions of people around you to successes and things that go wrong. They'll have opinions about speakers and judgements on whether to use certain spokespeople. Make notes. Take an interest. If the people around you get the impression that you are not interested, they'll pay you no attention. Make a good impression and ask if you can come back in the future.

At the other end of the work experience scale, some radio stations have very high expectations of the people they take on and, in return, they offer a very detailed programme of training. Kiss 100, for example, only wants second and third year university students. It wants those students to have some knowledge of sound editing and management and, preferably, experience with student radio.

Getting Work Experience

Virgin Radio wants people over 18 who have tried their hand at hospital or student radio. On its website it lists the qualities it is looking for:

Confident, reliable, self-motivated, and prepared to make the tea, sort the post, make the tea, answer the phones and make the tea on a daily basis in exchange for getting to do some really fun stuff like popping out to ask people in the street silly questions, making the tea,

There are many alternatives but here's one suggestion. Write for your school, college or university newspaper. There are also local papers and free weeklies that can be picked up in street magazine dispensers. You can call the marketing department of a publishing company and ask for a book that interests you. (Books on goddess therapy were big when I was at college!) Say that you are going to write a review and that you'll send a copy of the article for their records. You could call the local theatre and ask for a press ticket to see a play for the purposes of reviewing it.

Calling and requesting is a skill that you will rely upon in your radio career. Many programmes hinge on the producer and researcher's 'cold calling' skills for requesting books, tickets, interviewees – celebrities, politicians and other interesting types – for the programme content. Telephone charm is essential.

Always sound professional and in charge. Make sure the tone of your voice conveys confidence. You don't have to sound like the military but you must not sound limp. If you are asked for some information that you don't have, say: 'I'll check and get straight back to you.' There's no reason for you to have an apologetic voice or to sound like you don't know what you're doing: the producer you finally work with must be able to trust you with the phone work.

Anyway, you can start by filling the pages of your school/college newspaper with reviews and articles. This will get you used to calling up press offices, making your case, and writing. Not many schools and colleges are lucky enough to have their own radio station. In the meantime, get working and get into print.

If, in the future, you decide to do a university or postgraduate media course you may well be asked for your 'cuttings' or for a sound reel. You must keep all your published articles and keep a copy of anything you do that is broadcast.

and participating on-air. Except we can't promise that it'll be fun. Or that you'll get on-air. Or that you'll even get to make the tea.

The BBC also has a very detailed work experience web page: www.bbc.co.uk/jobs/workexperience_hub.shtml.

Also take a look at the *Work Placement Digest* on the Commercial Radio Companies Association site (www.crca.co.uk). You'll find the digest in pdf format, in the *Working in Radio* section. This should help you to avoid sending speculative CVs and making hopeful phone calls to stations that only deal with colleges or never offer work experience placements.

Is this a little too fast? Ok, take a step back. We need to build up confidence and knowledge as we proceed through this book.

WHAT DOES IT TAKE TO GET STARTED?

This is my story. I signed up for an evening class, which was a three-hour session on a Monday night, for five weeks. My first teacher was Owen Bennett Jones who is a BBC correspondent and can be heard on the World Service sending despatches from all kinds of troubled countries.

After four weeks on this course I was bitten by the radio bug. I went to New York and bought myself a Marantz. I came home and phoned theatres, national and fringe, and got myself free press passes to see plays. I organised, through the various press officers, to interview actors or directors. I gained access to editing facilities at BBC LDN 94.9FM (which was GLR at the time) and broadcast my packages on festival radio stations such as Notting Hill Carnival radio. I never felt so alive!

Checklist

Don't get bogged down with too much information! Are you getting a clearer idea of the field or is it just getting too complex and overwhelming? Are you getting an idea of how to proceed? Let's do a little review. Tick off tasks as you go along.

What have you done so far?

- Retuned your radio? Again and again?
- Written down your reasons for wanting a career in radio?
- Thought about the types of radio and where you would like to fit in?
- Used the Internet to find out about your favourite presenters or radio station?
- Found out about your local hospital radio?
- Looked at the Community Radio and Student Radio websites?
- Logged on to the Royal Academy website? Become a member?

What have you decided to do?

- Ask your lecturer/careers adviser/teacher for advice?
- Choose your GCSE, A-level or degree subjects?
- Write for a publication?
- Fix a work experience placement?

'Record your voice, your interviews and your sound effects and create something broadcastable!'

tools of the trade

Des Shepherd has worked in radio as a managing director, a freelance presenter, and a consultant. I wrote to him for advice in his capacity as someone who runs radio training courses (www.broadcasttraining.co.uk). Some radio stations and training studios are going to be better equipped than others, so I asked him what you should expect to find.

This is what he said:

Des Shepherd

Much of the radio industry has now gone digital. Studios have a mixer and hard disc playout system (RCS Master Control for example). Talk stations and newsrooms may use a hard disc system called Burli – this is also a RCS product. Even BBC local radio has developed its own hard disc system called Radioman. Open reel tape is no longer used. Basic radio studios would have CDs.

Colleges tend to lag behind and often have basic equipment – mixer, CDs, MiniDiscs and a computer for edited work. Most colleges tend to use Cool Edit Pro – a professional system as used by the BBC and many commercial stations. Cool Edit has replaced open reel tape machines as an editing tool and has the advantage that you can multi-track on it. Often used for making commercials, features or even whole programmes.

More progressive training centres would have a hard disc system – and universities might well be better resourced with top of the range hard disc systems.

Uhers are history – most location recording is done on MiniDiscs – difficult to name names as new models appear almost weekly. Marantzs still tend to be used, both on training courses and in the industry but MiniDiscs are the way of the future.

,,

GLOSSARY

Let's go through some of these terms.

HARD DISC SYSTEM

You can find out a lot about different RCS systems from their website (www.rcsuk.com/). The BBC systems are, of course, similar. As long as you are PC literate you'll be fine with these. Here's a taster of what you will find on the RCS website:

Selector, they say on their website, is radio's best known, and most widely used music scheduler to manage their music rotation. The *Burli* newsroom system integrates text and audio on one screen. It can take both wire services and network audio feeds. You can be working on a script and audio at the same time at your desk.

The *TalkBack* system keeps a history of each person's call to the station. As soon as a caller rings the station, their details are displayed on the phone-ops screen. The presenter or phone-op can grade each caller's performance and type in a comment immediately after the call. The system also gives access to news stories, newspaper clippings, actuality, helpline numbers and Internet pages stored in the *TalkBack* Organiser.

RECORDING EQUIPMENT

The *Uher*, as Des says, is history, but you might come across this beautiful museum piece sitting on its lonesome in a corner somewhere. Recording was on open reel-to-reel tape. This was liberated from the cumbersome machine and put onto a cutting machine – possibly a Revox. Tape was marked with a chalk pencil, cut with a razor and put back together with invisible tape. Disused tape made a lot of mess. The World Service employed people just for 'tape reclamation', which meant sticking discarded tape together for reuse!

Sony's latest MZ-N910 MiniDisc is a fiddly little thing and made me think of my own training on a *Marantz*, which couldn't be more simple to use and the chances of deleting your own work are too slim to mention. The only mistake you can make on a Marantz is to forget to switch from 'Tape' to 'Source' and deafen yourself with the feedback – which is quite funny. Otherwise, you learn about setting your levels and avoiding 'mic rattle', and you're away!

The MiniDisc needs more vigilance otherwise you will record over your masterpiece interviews. (I used a MiniDisc to interview Anthea Turner once ... and then again just five minutes later! She was terribly gracious and said all the same things again as if delivering her thoughts for the first time!) However, the industry is all in a tizz about the MiniDisc recorder and it has to be mastered. They are expensive so don't rush out and buy. On the other hand, they are cheap compared to the money I spent on my Marantz in 1995 – I think $400.

The MiniDisc is a tiny piece of equipment and, for the rough and tumble of professional life, radio engineers have designed a 'conversion kit' for its protection, which can be found in the workplace.

If you're lucky enough to have one or get one as a present then start interviewing friends and family to get used to the functions. Make your recordings then follow the instruction book for the editing and labelling functions of the MiniDisc. You can also record from the TV or radio (strictly for your own use) to practise. For this you will need an extra *cable*. Any good electrical shop will sell it. You can use the same cable to download your recordings onto a PC, which will go from your *line out* (on the MZ-N910 that's the same as the headphone socket) to the PC *line in*.

You have to buy a microphone separately but if you have an earpiece attachment from your mobile phone, that works. I had a go with mine and all you'll need is an extra jack (a small adapter plug) again from the electrical shop for less than £1.

Sony produces a Uni Directional Electret Condenser Microphone. I warn you that this costs approximately £60 but it is a little thing of beauty! It looks like something James Bond would have as a secret weapon. It's the size of a jack and comes with a mic windshield.

You'll learn that you have to hold the mic about a span's width from your interviewee's mouth. This is to avoid sibilance from 's's and popping from 'p's. The mic windshield will also lessen these effects. You'll also learn that you can't just launch into an interview without asking a meaningless question in order to set up your levels and listen back to the voice of your interviewee. You must double check, on the spot, that everything is in working order. A normal question for this purpose is 'What did you have for breakfast?' (The answer is never very interesting!)

I found that, if the MiniDisc battery wasn't fully charged, you hear the internal workings of the MiniDisc making a whirring noise. You either need to make sure you have fully charged batteries or use the mains plug.

The other thing you'll learn is that, as you are recording, you must be listening through headphones – whether using a MiniDisc or Marantz. Otherwise you'll find, too late, that you have popping and whirring and noises from your mic cable or hand movements and no possibility of repeating the interview. (The MiniDisc will be sensitive to any movement from your hand so, while recording, you have to be very still.)

The best way to learn is to experiment. Even, better, join a training organisation that will lend you equipment and can guide you when you are ready to buy. The electrical support department on my postgraduate course sold MiniDiscs that had been 'converted' for journalists' use. Training organisations at all levels will either offer this or will be able to suggest alternatives.

SOUND EDITING PACKAGES
On my PC at home I've got Cool Edit Pro and Pro Tools. Both of these are commonly used in the workplace. Cool Edit can be downloaded for something like £35. Go to www.syntrillium.com for more information. Pro Tools is an industry standard and can be downloaded for free: www.protools.com. You can also download lots of instruction information such as their Quick Start and Reference Guides. Both of these digital editing packages turn a PC into a recording studio. If you master one you'll be fine with others.

If you see your future in this area and you want to be an editor extraordinaire of trails, adverts, and really creative jobs, SADiE is the tool with the biggest name in the industry. (There are over 600 SADiE systems in use throughout the BBC.) You can download their latest system if you have Windows 2000 or XP from www.sadie.com.

I've worked with all of these systems with very little workplace training. With Pro Tools I had the privilege at BBC Radio 1 to work on trails beside a professional, full-time editor who worked like a charm and created a dream out of my clips and cuttings and vague ideas.

Record your voice, your interviews and your sound effects and create something broadcastable! Your finished product could be burnt onto a CD, posted on your website or emailed to friends.

RECORD DECKS
They disappeared from radio stations, largely overtaken by CDs and hard-disk systems but recently made a comeback on certain stations like Kiss100. 1Xtra will use its record decks pretty much continuously on air to mix its output.

BUY OR BORROW?

If you are working as a volunteer in a radio station you will have access to some or all of these things and you may be able to borrow recording equipment. If you have a computer at home you can get a sound card and editing package. If you don't have money to invest in having your own equipment, it really shouldn't be a problem.

I recommend that, instead of buying your own equipment, you take the option of finding a training centre where you can borrow theirs. There are many privileges that go along with this. You'll have advice and support on tap. You'll be in a positive environment. The training centre will be aware of RSLs in the area. You'll have a ready-made team to work with. You'll learn to work with others and respect the needs of others. Always be aware of the needs of your colleagues.

This is also where you can start a career of effective networking. Keep in touch with your fellow trainees and share tips and contacts that come your way. As you all move into the industry you'll appreciate each other's support. Your training centre may invite teachers from the industry – make good use of their time and advice and keep contact details. While you're looking out for people who might be useful to you, make sure you are someone who is worth networking with as well. Help others whenever you get the opportunity.

STUDIO PRODUCER

Do you want to follow a technical career? Even if you don't, you'll need to understand the 'desk' and you'll probably use it, whatever your job title is. Otherwise you'll be working closely with someone like Ola French who *drives the desk* on Radio London 94.9FM on the Danny Baker show.

Ola French: Studio Manager

The Danny Baker Show is a breakfast show that contains witty studio chat with two sidekicks, guests and listeners' calls. The programme includes breaks for news and travel and has music 'beds', which are played underneath the presenter's voice at points – perhaps as the programme comes out of the news or underneath a feature. There are no pre-recorded pieces.

What does it mean to drive a desk?

Ola: 'Driving' is just another word for 'operating'. The mixing desk that I use is a 'virtual desk' consisting of 12 faders (six on my left hand side, six on my right), six computer screens, one 'Callstar' phone unit, three studio monitors (speakers), one talkback box (this enables me to talk to the producer presenter travel and news reader and the news editor), two CD players, one Dat machine, two MiniDisc players, two turntables, three microphones and a pair of headphones.

Why is it called a desk?

Ola: It's called a desk because it is simply that: it's a mixing desk and it's like any office desk that you sit and work at. This one has just a few more electronic toys to play with. I set it up as I want and save the settings on the computer for the programme I work on.

What do you do during a programme?

Ola: My job starts before the programme because I have to check that microphones, headphones and desk settings are all set up. Each show has its own settings and when a new presenter starts you have to work it all out from scratch. For example, you get them to chat on the mic to get their 'level' which is saved and recalled every time they are presenting.

During the programme I am responsible for the output of the programme. I fade up the microphones, the callers, play all the jingles and, if it's a music-based programme, CDs as well. Whatever you hear coming out of your radio set, I'm the one who has triggered or fired it in.
During the programme I also have to keep a close ear to the output, and knowledge of the law (slander, defamation and accusations) is a must. This is strictly the producer's job but, when push comes to shove, you can't say you didn't know or didn't hear.

Where did you get your training?

Ola: You can be trained on the job but the BBC does a full and comprehensive training course, teaching the complete workings of the desk and knowledge of how radio works.

The programme depends on you completely. Is this a highly pressurised job?

Ola: It can be but the trick is to always be a step ahead and get to know how your fellow workers react to different situations.

What happens when things go wrong?

Ola: When things go belly up that is the time when you need to keep your head. Most things can easily be corrected within a few seconds once the problem is found.

What do you like about the job?

Ola: Many things! I work on the breakfast show, which is fun. There are different guests every day and entertaining stories from callers. Where else do you laugh for three hours and get paid for it?

What made you decide on this career?

Ola: I've always had a love for radio.

Do you have to have training in journalism?

Ola: No, but knowledge of law is essential.

Do you get involved in setting up the programme and organising guests?

Ola: Yes. New ideas are always needed.

'Keep a radio diary and make notes on what you find interesting, the techniques you noticed, the styles you enjoy.'

the realities of the job

WHAT IS A PACKAGE?

The best way of finding out is to listen to the 'Today' programme on Radio 4. Sorry about that if you're a budding music radio maestro but retune, for a while, to R4. Once you've listened to the R4 way of cutting a package you'll recognise the form on other programmes.

A package is a three-minute-or-so recording containing these elements: an introduction, atmosphere (sometimes called 'atmos'), interviews with perhaps two or three people ('clips' or short recordings that may be taken on location or perhaps on the phone) and script (links voiced by the reporter) to pull it all together.

Sit by your radio with a notebook. When you hear the introduction to a package, make some notes. (You'll hear the studio presenter give an introduction to the package which includes the words, 'We sent our reporter, So And So, to find out,' or 'So And So reports,' or some such hand-over.)

Listen out for how the presenter leads into the package. How does the package itself start? Is it with the reporter's voice, straight into a sound effect or straight into a clip? Note the timing of the introduction and links. What is the timing of each clip? Are they interview exchanges, vox pops, or comments? Listen to how the journalist's links pull you from one clip to another and create the dynamic to take you through the story. How does the journalist wrap up the subject? How long was the package in total?

Listen to the content and the balance of script versus interview. Listen to the use of background noise – the atmosphere. Judge how it enhanced the story or the background of the news they gave you. Did it help or hinder your understanding of the subject? From now on when you listen to your radio, keep a radio diary and make notes on what you find interesting, the techniques you noticed, the styles you enjoy.

Make notes, also, of things you disapprove of. I've listened to features on Sri Lanka where Indian music has been used. I've listened to hundreds of news pieces from African countries that are dressed up with market noises and women singing. Does a whole continent really only ever sing and go to market? Stories from Buddhist countries that are accompanied by monks' chanting annoy me! Are stories from Christian countries accompanied by hymns?

As a radio journalist, think about what flavour you would give to different topics and how you would find the atmos to deliver it. Are you endorsing a stereotype or are you painting an accurate picture? You must be sincere and pay respect to the subject you're tackling.

But once you get the package format under your belt you'll be able to produce whole programmes that are beautifully mixed and edited with colourful voices, creative sound effects and brilliantly layered audio, all of which will pull your listeners' ears off the sides of their heads and attach them to the radio!

Here's an example of a package script written by Roger Harrabin, a correspondent for the 'Today' programme on BBC Radio 4. It's about the vote in Poland on joining the European Union, which the presenter in the studio explains in the introduction. He has written 'FX' for sound effects in his script and he has used clips of interviews with workers and a hairdresser, which are also marked in the script.

Look at how it flows. Look at how his links lead you from one interview to another and look at how he's used sound effects. The end of the report would have been the studio presenter saying something like: 'And that was Roger Harrabin reporting from Gdansk' for the back announcement.

Script

The Polish people go to the ballot box today to decide if they'll join the European Union. If they say yes it'll bring in a pool of 18 million workers. It'll also bring a state regarded by France and Germany as being the most pro-American of a generally pro-American bunch of accession states. Our correspondent Roger Harrabin has been gauging the public mood.

FX bulldozer

I'm standing next to a wildlife reserve near Gdansk in northern Poland. The scene seems to capture some of the mood in the country at the moment. There's a dash for economic growth that's pretty careless about its consequences. Behind me bulldozers are levelling a hill so the local parish council can cash in with a private housing estate. The big work's done by machines –

FX stones

but as if to prove the economy is still in transition, the workers are hauling stones by hand off a horse-drawn cart. There's a feeling of energy and optimism about the place. And most of the workers here feel that their future lies with the west.

Workers

FX hairdresser

The centre of Gdansk – remembered in the UK as the birthplace of the Solidarity movement – now looks like the handsome and prosperous German port that it once was. Elegantly restored buildings interspersed with bland shopping malls like this one where the hairdresser gave the sort of answer about Poland's future place in Europe that I heard many times.

Hairdresser

I'll vote yes for my children, she says. Not for me but for my children's future.

FX birds

But that's in a city that made its money trading with the West.

In rural areas there's religious conservatism among some Poles who believe western Europe with its tolerance of abortion and homosexuality a sinful place.

Many of Poland's old peasant farmers live in fear that European agricultural subsidies will ruin their jobs and their way of life.

Farmer Henryk

FX university

But even farmers are apparently split, with some prepared to trade off their own present losses against hoped-for future benefits for their children and grandchildren – people like the students here at Gdansk University. Zhjislav Brodetski professor of euro law says the spirit of self-sacrifice abounds.

Professor

FX school

And here is Poland's future – the sixth form at Gdansk Number Two grammar school. There's no doubt about where these youngsters are heading.

Girls x3

Roger question

Farmer Henryk

End

So, when you listen out for radio packages, listen to how the correspondent has taken you from the introduction, into a picture that distils the story, into interviews that back up a theme, into sound effects that bring life to the piece, into a conclusion that sums up the mood.

I took this script and showed it to Andy Brown, a broadcast journalist with 'Newsbeat' at BBC Radio 1 and 1Xtra, the BBC digital station dedicated to black and urban music.

When 1Xtra was recruiting before the launch of the station, its emphasis was on finding people with an encyclopaedic knowledge of black and urban music. Andy's background is different. He started at the award-winning University of Essex radio, moved to the highly respected Vauxhall Radio Studio at Lambeth College in London, then to FLR radio station, then to London's News Direct, then to work in radio at SBS in Sydney while travelling, then to 'Newsbeat'. He says it took four years to get from his college course to this job – his dream job.

His reaction to the Radio 4 script was as I expected: it's a format he couldn't use. To cut a package for Radio 1's 'Newsbeat', which is a 15-minute bulletin, the style has to be tight and fit into one and a half minutes. This means all superfluous words are brutally edited out. The package will include two or three speakers, sound effects and extremely short links.

At 1Xtra the news bulletin is an hour long and it mixes news packages with music – it's not a straight news programme – so a package can be three minutes long and can be in a more laid-back style to reflect the personality of the station.

In both cases the links are interesting. They couldn't be more unlike the Radio 4 style, where they serve the purpose of leading from one idea to another and introducing the next speaker. Newsbeat use links more like 'teasers'.

Here's an example: if the package includes a recorded quote from the subject's mother then the link after the clip might be, 'That was her mum'. Then into the next quote, followed by the link, 'and that was her dad'. It nudges you through the interview clips in a very conversational way. The style really strains at the leash of the standard, traditional format. Andy says that it's like listening to your mates talking, which doesn't describe the Polish story at all. Listen out for both.

Here's something else to consider with the Radio 1 and 1Xtra style. Audience research shows that the age range of their audience is wider than even they expected. Instead of being able to simply write for the teenage market, Andy and his colleagues find that they are writing for people from 10 years old to 30. Audience research shows the time the different listeners tune in and for how long. A 'Newsbeat' package about schools captured the 14-18-year-old market. The entire age range listened to a piece about Posh and Becks. The older section of the audience listened to news about Iraq. The challenge, of course, is to write for all the listeners.

INTERVIEWS – THE LIFEBLOOD OF RADIO

In speech radio, or wherever guests and interviews occur, all of the production team will have some responsibility for preparing the programme, including getting the research and writing done.

Here is a question asked on many courses on radio production: name the top ten people you want to interview. So be prepared. Think about the people you look up to. Nelson Mandela was always a favourite feature of this list but if you choose him, remember that he's been interviewed an infinite number of times since his release from jail. There can't be many questions he hasn't answered over and over again.

With all interviews, try to discover what you can ask that no other journalist has asked. How can you make your interview stand above the rest? What will be different about your approach? Have you done your research? Have you read enough to be sufficiently informed on the subject? What's your angle?

Some authors and film stars always take their places on the list. Here's a task for you: choose your top ten – anyone from the biggest star of the moment to the aromatherapist at the local gym. Write a series of questions. Jot down a brief line or two about what you imagine the answer to be. Then write down what links you would write to edit these pieces together. Your script must, of course, include a scintillating introduction to the subject and an authoritative or entertaining conclusion.

Here's another task: write down the bottom ten people you can imagine having to interview. What characters are you really not interested in? (Mine would all be footballers!) Repeat the task above: the questions, a brief imagined answer, and the script that will link your clips together.

This will take more research and more creativity on your part to make it into a quality interview. Your package will be listened to by people who love the person you're interviewing and adore the topic and they will probably spend their lives reading about it.

For this you have to know who to turn to for help, what organisations to call, and how to ask for a hand in taking you through the subject. You need to do a pre-interview interview to find out what questions to ask! Don't worry, you can't be expected to know everything, but don't ever be dismissive and do a half-baked job.

In the workplace you would ask for your colleagues' help. If they are all busy you could find a contact for a fan club, an agent or PR person. When tackling a subject that you are unfamiliar with and when seeking help, be clear about what it is you are asking for. Say that this is not your area of expertise and you want to find the best interview questions possible. You will probably find that everyone you speak to wants to achieve a good quality interview.

If you are talking to a fan or an agent, they'll be passionate about the subject and will either give you guidance or tell you the best place to go for help. If they don't offer the help then ask for a recommendation for an alternative contact.

Here are some of my dream interviews and my reasons. Practise your writing and research skills with this list. You and your script have to produce the most interesting, wittiest and most 'unswitchoffable' radio:

- Cyclist Lance Armstrong (I love cycling)
- Photographer Sabastiao Salgado (My favourite photographer)
- Shoe designer Manolo Blahnik (What a great exhibition)
- Laila Ali, Mohammed Ali's daughter (I've taken up boxing. Could do with tips)
- Designer Paul Smith (He loves cycling too)
- Violinist Vanessa Mae (I play violin in an amateur orchestra, not like her though!)
- Poet Jonathan Agard (On writing for children. My next ambition.)

The reason behind writing down an imagined answer is that, quite literally, you will already know what answer or angle will be given. You research will have given you that. It's rare that a journalist is caught completely unawares and without a follow-up question prepared. You'll have your list of questions, you'll know the direction each answer will lead into and how your next question will neatly follow on. It sounds contrived but it's up to you to make it attention-grabbing.

WHEN THINGS GO WRONG

Take a look on the BBC website at Nicky Campbell's studio discussion with Will Self and Richard Littlejohn. It's a joy to read. Both of the guests had recently published books. Nicky Campbell hadn't read either. This is a studio discussion nightmare waiting to happen. Put 'Will Self v Richard Littlejohn' into the search engine and take a look. The full address is: http://news.bbc.co.uk/1/hi/uk/1390395.stm.

Some producers will not give full questions to their presenters in the fear that the presenter won't read up on the subject properly. Instead, the producer will write an introduction and provide background notes. Each presenter has particular needs and demands. In an interview on the BBC website, Mark Lawson says that he will only ever read his own scripts.

THE UNEXPECTED INTERVIEW

There's only so much a researcher or producer can do. The presenter, with his or her sparkling personality and ready wit, is the one who takes the ultimate responsibility for turning an interview into compelling listening. But try, in your suggested questions, to take the listener on an unexpected journey.

There are the standard questions and there are the usual answers. If you flick through your radio channels you'll hear celebrities who do the media junket when, for example, promoting a book or a film. You'll then turn on the TV and hear the same questions and the same answers, quips, phrases, jokes and sensational revelations. But doesn't your guest have a personality that is bigger than his or her public persona? To find the unexpected in every interview is difficult so don't underestimate the task. Listen out for examples of presenters using an interviewee well.

I remember a very entertaining interview that Steve Wright did with Whitney Houston. He asked about her child and they shared experiences of the school run. He asked about how she trained her voice and what voice exercises she did, so she gave a demonstration which was a very strange, gurgling, throaty sound.

Then during a break in the interview when he was playing a track he primed her to answer some questions about 'EastEnders' and football. When they came back after the music she had some strangely detailed opinions about the plot of 'EastEnders' and what Ricky should have done, and some views on the transfer market and who one of the premier teams should be looking to buy. It was so against the expectation of the listener, such a surprise, so light, such a cosy chat, and very creative on Steve's part.

The Simon Mayo afternoon show on BBC Radio 5 Live happened upon a lovely interview with Patrick Stewart and had him reading the 2.20pm Five Live Travel. Patrick Stewart was obviously enthusiastic to be in front of the radio mic. His voice was deep velvet. It was infectious.

He called himself a 'child of the radio'. He said his first contact with news, drama and entertainment as a child was through radio; it remains his first port of call for this information. He loves radio and he wanted to read the travel news. The listener could enjoy the image of a costumed and made-up Captain Jean-Luc Picard or Ebenezer Scrooge or Professor Charles Xavier (pick one of his many characters) while hearing about a chemical spillage in Shropshire, an incident in Oxfordshire and about junctions and A roads. It was compelling.

If you want to go into a news career, don't think that the unexpected journey with humour and imagination is not part of your remit. On BBC Radio Five Live Stephen Byers, when he was education minister, was asked an eight-times-table question and blurted out the wrong answer. It was nice to hear him criticising the paucity of knowledge students are leaving school with and then slip up like that. Politically insignificant, really, but nice radio!

On Five Live again, sports minister Richard Caborn was asked five simple questions about mainstream sport, on sporting events taking place and sporting personalities in the news. Guess what – he couldn't answer a thing. At a different level, George Bush, when campaigning for the American presidency, was asked the names of heads of state and famously didn't know any. It was an utter pleasure to listen to.

Some ministers, anyway, ignore the journalist's question and answer an alternative, imagined question that is tailored to the answer they want to give. There is a recent trend for political pundits and press conference speakers to ask themselves questions and then answer them: 'Do I think ABC, well, no I don't. Would I do XYZ, well, yes, I would. Will I be meeting with so-and-so, well, that depends on ABC.' What a cheek! How can you get in there and puncture the inflated ego? Your creativity and distinctive approach are crucial, as you can see.

Checklist

Another review.

What have you done so far?

- Started a radio diary?
- Listened to and studied packages on radio?
- Practised your writing skills?
- Made contacts?
- Looked at the suggested websites?

What will you do next?

- Write for a school or college newspaper?
- Organise work experience?
- Contact a radio station?
- Gain access to equipment?

'Concern yourself with writing that is stamped with your personality and enthusiasm and your best attempt at a fresh angle.'

fact, fiction and straight writing

The editorial meeting is when everyone involved with producing the programme will thrash out ideas and form the programme. Before the meeting everyone will have gone through the tabloid and broadsheet newspapers. Much of the booking of guests will have been done by 'forward planning', so most of the programme will be in place but the topical bits, the newsworthy items, suggestions of questions to ask the guests or new angles on their subject will be offered and completely new ideas can be tendered.

At its best, the editorial meeting is an exciting brainstorming session. Always take in loads of ideas with you, even if you don't use them all. Always have something to suggest with back-up research and possible speakers on the subject. Always say why it would be compelling listening. Say why it would suit the audience profile of the programme.

Here's an example. There is a new anti-wrinkle treatment. If you suggest this topic, you'll need to say why it will be entertaining or controversial. If it includes injecting something without evidence of long-term side effects, you're on to a winner. If it's a treatment that has been withdrawn from the market in another country then you're on to a scandal.

Potential guests include someone who has had the treatment and recommends it, another for whom it went wrong, the person/doctor who discovered the treatment or someone from his or her company, someone from the Patients' Association, a representative of plastic or cosmetic surgeons or a Harley Street doctor, someone from the Medical Control Association, someone from the Food and Drug Administration in America to give the US perspective. As you can see, there are plenty of angles.

Back up your ideas with lots of suggestions. The more you have to offer, the more sources you speak to, the richer your writing will be.

STRAIGHT WRITING

Some subjects won't allow you to be witty. You just have to dig through the details and inform the listener. Here's one that is as straight as a ruler. It has an introduction, suggested questions, and, where the presenter needs to know what the question is based on, notes in brackets.

GM FOOD Steve Wright, 13 March 1999

Steve Wright makes the introduction:

Fast-food outlets are turning their backs on genetically modified. Supermarkets are being challenged to disclose the ingredients of 'own brand' products. The government is under pressure to give answers on GM safety and labelling. But what do ordinary people think? My guests are Steve Jones, professor of genetics at the University College London and Robin Maynard, local campaign director for Friends of the Earth.

The first few questions set up the subject: what exactly is GM food, is it just another food scare story, what are the potential benefits, potential dangers, how prevalent are GM foods in the food chain and how long have we been eating this stuff? What about the subject of GM food as an aid to the starving in underdeveloped countries?

What else do you think the listener wants to know? Do they want to hear about the science of cross-pollination and modifying genes? Do they want to know if GM food is a scandal in the making? Does the consumer care?

With good background reading the presenter will be able to deliver such questions and conduct a thoughtful studio discussion.

More specific questions need back-up notes on the script:

Steve Wright, question to Steve Jones: *the issue blew up recently because of Dr Pusztai. Take us through what that was all about.*

(Dr Pusztai claimed the animals used in one experiment showed slight growth retardation, an effect on the immune system and changes in the weight of their internal organs. Dr Pusztai was accused of confusing the results and releasing data not yet in the public domain.)

Was there an effort to gag him?

(Dr Pusztai described to the House of Commons committee how Rowett Research Institute Professor James wrote to him giving his guidelines on 'what he could or could not do' following the controversy.)

SW asks Robin Maynard: *what about controls to protect crops from cross-pollination by genetically-modified plants? Is this where the real concern should be?*

(Dr Jean Emberlin, Director of the National Pollen Research Unit, has produced evidence to show that pollen from maize can be dispersed over much greater distances than has been accepted by government scientists. At present, a 200-metre 'exclusion zone' is set up around a GM maize crop undergoing trials and is considered a sufficient barrier to prevent cross-contamination of ordinary maize crops or sweet corn. But Dr Emberlin, whose research was commissioned by the Soil Association, says bees or strong winds will take the pollen much further. She believes the government should now stop the controversial large-scale cultivation of GM crops, which is planned to start in a matter of weeks.)

And so on.

This is an example of researching a topic that I was unfamiliar with. I got hours of help from the organisations I called. The people who finally came on the programme as guests also phoned me for long conversations on the complexities of the issue. They couldn't have been more willing or have given more time.

WHAT? WHY? WHO? WHEN? WHERE?

A common job interview question is, 'What would you say in an introduction to ...'. In an instant, you'll have to show that your knowledge of the person or subject is up to date, that you can home in on the most germane points and that you have an entertaining turn of phrase and a way with words.

Practise. Make use of your radio diary. Write introductions to everything. If you're stuck for a starting point try the What? Why? Who? When? Where? approach. An extra, key, question that doesn't fit so neatly into the row of 'W's is 'How?' The point is that you are trying to pick out the most interesting, the most topical and the most up-to-date piece of information to offer the listener first. Everything else comes along to back up that information and give it more substance.

When you are listening to presenters give their introductions on radio, run it by this list and see how they've used, or not used, these questions. Take a look at the interviews I've included in this book and see if there's anything I've missed.

Avoid closed questions such as, 'Do you think XYZ?' The answer might be 'Yes' or 'No', which isn't very detailed or interesting.

Always reread your work and read it out aloud to see if the rhythm of your words work. Have you overused words or repeated adjectives? Are sentences too long and unwieldy? Have you made a simple idea complex or rendered a complex idea as dull as dishwater? Is the true meaning conveyed or confused? Explain yourself, some advise, as if you're talking to your grandmother.

On top of all this, it's got to be interesting and entertaining. Is your piece compelling or does it 'lack the gong-like clash of spontaneous enthusiasm' (from Ernest Bramah, *The Story of Hein and the Chief Examiner*)? You must try to enjoy the vocabulary you employ. Be elegant in your style without being condescending or laborious. Speak well and write well. 'Wah'ever, wah'ever' is not a substitute for finishing a sentence. 'An' evryfing' is not a substitute for concluding an idea.

FACT AND FICTION

Keep away from generalisations, don't copy the words or ideas of others, be proud of your original, well-researched work. Be specific – or become a storyteller rather than a journalist. To be any kind of reporter means that you are taking a fact from point A and delivering it to point B. Don't be lazy or make up information in the middle of the process. People will turn off in their droves or, at the very least, you will have introduced your topic in a way that annoys people and makes them dismissive of everything that will follow.

I once heard an education correspondent start a report with, 'We all want the best for our little darlings.' I wonder where he's been during the recent rise in exclusions, the first ever jailing of a mother for not ensuring her child's education and all those teachers' conferences where they bemoan the hostility of parents. And, besides, do we all have 'little darlings'? I'm not a parent. Don't generalise. It annoys discerning listeners.

Here are a couple of things I've noted in the newspaper.

'May you live in interesting times' is not, in fact, an ancient Chinese curse. According to the experts, the only Chinese proverb that comes close says, 'It's better to be a dog in a peaceful time than a man in a chaotic time'.

Who on earth are these experts? 'According to experts' is a phrase that is over-employed and it always makes me think that the writer is guessing and hasn't done much research or made many phone calls. The 'interesting times' example is quite an innocent example (taken from the May/June 2003 issue of *Mother Jones*, an Internet news website) but listen out for all the unnamed experts. I especially detest 'According to civil liberty groups' when I suspect they're only talking about one group, Liberty.

'Parents are paying nearly £50,000 extra to buy a home in the catchment area of a good local primary school in England.'

Daily Telegraph, 30 May 2003

Can it be true that all parents in the UK have such a large extra wedge of money? This doesn't describe my parents, or the parents of anyone I know.

You already know that plagiarising is intellectual theft and, in any case, is a ridiculous thing to do. Don't ever steal. The University of Newcastle website gives this definition: 'Plagiarism is an attempt to pass someone else's work as your own. This is a serious offence and may result in disciplinary measures being taken against anyone who is found to be plagiarising.'

On the other hand, I have heard long-in-the-tooth radio people say that there's no such thing as a new story. Freelance programme writers might worry, when sending a script to a production company, that the idea will be stolen. My opinion is that this doesn't really happen. I've heard people worry about it but never heard a story of an actual grievance. I think any production company would argue that it is not in their interest, nor is it practical or logical, to steal like this. Instead of worrying about this you can concern yourself with writing that is stamped with your personality and enthusiasm and your best attempt at a fresh angle. If you are sending ideas to a production company, make a proper contact and don't send stories on spec.

Whether reporting the news or scripting a feature programme, you can apply intellect and honesty to the smallest and greatest of stories.

'Many of the young people who approach me and say they want to get into radio, TV or journalism have no notion of what is required. It's scary.'

getting into good habits

I've asked all the contributors to this book for advice to inspire and point the way into the industry.

Henry Bonsu is a broadcaster on BBC LDN 94.9, a Channel 5 panellist on 'The Right Stuff' and a director of The Creative Collective (www.thecreativecollective.com).

Henry is, as are the other contributors, someone who loves his craft and who has a vast general knowledge that he delights in putting to use in his interviews. He also puts a lot of time into helping people learn about the industry by giving talks in the community. However, I thought I'd ask him for a different angle: what annoys him about today's radio wannabes. It was hours before we got off the phone! Here's a summary of what he said:

Many of the young people who approach me and say they want to get into radio, TV or journalism have no notion of what is required. It's scary.

If you want to work in the business you must learn how to communicate verbally and in writing. You cannot communicate in 'spit slang'. It will restrict your market. English is the most accessible language in the world. For linguistic and historical reasons it's the most widely spoken language in the world. If you have the benefit of speaking English as your birthright, learn to speak it properly.

'Spit slang' may be fine for signing a record deal but in other environments you will be horrendously embarrassed. Every job you go for will require you to be confident and speak clearly. If you can't finish your sentence you'll be at the back of the queue. Open you mouth and speak clearly. If the person on the other end of the phone doesn't respect you, they won't help you. If you can't communicate then your chances of progressing are limited. **"**

Sound your Ts through this chapter. There are things you should be doing as second nature by now. Let's review them.

GETTING INTO GOOD HABITS

COLLECT IDEAS
Take cuttings from newspapers and magazines. Keep an address book, not only for solid contacts but also for guest possibilities, whether you have the contact details yet or not. Make a note of why you would favour them as a guest. Always be ready for that editorial meeting where you'll be holding the attention of your colleagues and telling them about your interview or programme idea. Think about how to capture the imagination of the audience.

THINK ABOUT THE NEWS AGENDA
Think about the news stories of the day and how you would treat them. Who are the best speakers on the subject? Read the papers and memorise names. You may or may not agree with the choices made by the station you are listening to. You may get the impression that all news programmes chase the same contributors. How would you treat a firefighters' strike or the latest unemployment figures? (If you want to be a news reporter you should be building up knowledge of MPs' names, their departments, union leaders' names, representatives of charities and campaign organisations.)

Teachers of radio courses often do a news exercise that involves putting a number of stories into their order of importance. The idea is that the closer you are to making the choices actually made by the news programmes of the day, the closer you are to being 'right'. I could never bear this exercise but you should be prepared for it. While you're listening to the news, make a note of what the producer considered to be the lead story. Did you agree?

I once tried to lead a drive-time news programme with the story of an aeroplane crash in a little country. Plenty of people were killed and I didn't want to follow (what I thought was) the standard attitude that more important stories are from the more important countries. I worked long and hard at trying to get to the officials, trying to find someone to speak on air, and generally trying to get enough information and enough contributors to justify a lead story. It didn't work. I learnt that practicalities, not necessarily prejudices, might dictate the lead story.

RESEARCH EVERYTHING

If you like a presenter, look up their background. If you like a guest, find out more about them. When you read the papers or magazines, keep cuttings. If you hear a production company's name mentioned in the back-announcement of a programme you like, look it up. Sue Keogh from the production company Smooth Operations adds:

> You wouldn't believe the amount of people who come to us without any idea of what we do (for example a quick search on Google finds our website, which gives a brief outline on our homepage and then lists all our past and current productions). This is particularly unimpressive when it comes to employing people. The last time we interviewed, only one person had actually made the effort to find out what programmes we make and listen to them in advance.

BOOK BREAK

I came across a passage in Fi Glover's book (*I am an oil tanker: Travels with my radio*) that took me far away from my experience of turning on and tuning into my usual stations. It made me leave behind any preconceived ideas I have about the limitations of music radio and phone-in request shows. See what you think:

In Colombia there is a station that has, through the pressure of the listeners, created a programme that you are unlikely to find in any other part of the world. The late-night music show on Memories Radio started out as your average mellow phone-in request show but built up a strange momentum. Usually the point of a request show is obvious: you phone up and ask for a tune that makes you happy or makes you think of some important moment in your life. Maybe you might phone to ask for a tune to be played for someone else who is also listening. It is unlikely that you would request a tune in the hope that the person it is for is still alive.

But that's what the listeners of Memories started to do. More and more people called in wanting to play tunes for loved ones who had been kidnapped by the gangs who trade in human life. Now the switchboard gets jammed every night with people desperate to believe that they can reach out to whatever grotty, hellish room their father or wife or child has ended up in while they wait for the beleaguered and corrupt police force to try to find them.

THE BEGINNINGS OF RADIO

You can't proceed without knowing about Guglielmo Marconi, without whom there would be no possibility of this book or your radio career. (Yes, that may be an exaggeration, but some consider him to be the God of Radio.)

He proved, in 1897 at the age of 27, that 'wireless waves' would follow the curvature of the earth's surface. He then set about building a transmitter powerful enough to transmit across hundreds of miles and then across the Atlantic. Before this it was widely accepted that these wireless waves would travel only in a straight line from a transmitter to a receiver, without the interruption of hills and only to a place within the boundaries of the horizon.

Marconi and his team spent phenomenal amounts of money, built colossal machinery, made hopeful trips cross the Atlantic and suffered weather-inspired misfortunes to reach their day of victory when the letter 'S' was successfully transmitted in Morse code (dot dot dot). It may not sound like much now but, with that, the wonders of wireless telegraphy were born.

If you want to know more about this there is a very readable little book published by Marconi Communications called *Marconi's Atlantic Leap* by Gordon Bussey who is an authority on the subject.

Incidentally, Marconi and his wife Beatrice were invited to sail on the maiden voyage of the SS Titanic. But, for business reasons, Marconi had to leave earlier for New York on the Cunard line's SS Lusitania, while his wife had to cancel because Giulio, their baby son, was unwell. I got this information from a lovely website dedicated to Marconi: MarconiCalling.com (www.marconicalling.com/). You can order the book there.

'You'll also have the qualifications to show that you are the undiscovered brain of Britain.'

qualities you'll need

I asked Mark Simpson, a producer at Radio 2, to give an account of his entry into his radio career. You'll see that determination is possibly the most important ingredient.

If you are the kind of person who has an enquiring mind and is looking forward to the prospect of reading widely, informing yourself on a range of issues, supporting a presenter with well-researched information and the satisfaction of helping to broadcast good quality information, read on.

Mark will show you how varied a life in radio can be. At first you have to constantly put yourself forward to take opportunities. Recognition doesn't come easily, so see what you think of Mark's struggles and glories.

I listened to Mark present a programme on the night that Diana, Princess of Wales died. His programme was beautiful and sensitive; his mix of music and listeners' contributions was in perfect rhythm. His voice is soothing, like a pillow, and the programme was intelligent and fell into none of the traps of being mawkish or abusive of any listener's raw emotions.

His lifetime of reading, researching and listening makes him a producer and presenter with a clear idea of his approach and what will work, even in the most extreme of circumstances.

Mark Simpson: Producer at Radio 2

How did you start?

Mark: Got to be producer by luck and determination. I used to write film and music reviews at school for school magazines and fanzines, then met someone at a gig who asked me to go on his community radio show and talk about record releases and concerts.

After university I applied to the BBC and Independent London Radio (ILR) and got nowhere, but eventually got a voluntary job doing community slots at the local ILR station. Helped them out with a charity appeal and worked really hard for no payment. They offered me clerical jobs like writing travel bulletins and helping in the newsroom and eventually trained me as overnight presenter and producer.

I also worked in WH Smith and Virgin Megastores to keep up my interest in music and bring in some cash.

Then I moved around ILR until the BBC beckoned. Worked my way through local radio by doing anything that was available – writing, presenting, producing, researching everything from gardening shows, business specials, phone ins and flying-eye reports to music and news shows.

I had to start at the bottom again once I got into network radio as a BA. It stands for 'Broadcast Assistant' and is basically a glorified secretary but I just kept making suggestions and trying to get ideas commissioned.

What is it like to prepare a programme as a producer?

Mark: Read all the newspapers on a day-to-day basis. Check Internet sites like the BBC and Ananova. Listen to new records and read magazines like *Q, Empire* and *Harpers.* Go through all the incoming post and emails. Check the music selections for possibly offensive lyrics. Brief the presenter on any guests and significant news or station developments. Put in any last minute contributions like brand new records or things relevant to guest or breaking news story.

When the programme is on air, listen carefully to what the presenter is saying, help them with answers to questions, stumbles on air (via the talkback intercom), make quick decisions when necessary, time records to fit in the relevant time slots. Keep the presenter happy with jokes, compliments, cups of coffee, meet guests, brief them on interview content, listen out for libel, offence, swearing, etc.

Keep an eye on incoming phone calls, emails and texts and watch the news and Internet for breaking items. Make sure everything runs smoothly and that the listener is kept fully entertained and informed.

So exactly how did you train or was it on the job?

Mark: I tried to learn by listening to great broadcasters, reading training manuals and relevant autobiographies. Got proper training from experienced producers and presenters in ILR and then the BBC.

A degree is not essential, although I would try and get some form of further education and then do a course in broadcasting or studio techniques but only in addition to something else. I would not recommend doing only a media studies type degree. There are too many of these and they tend to be quite pretentious. The industry does not look as favourably on them as ordinary degrees. Many employers would rather someone had a degree in Maths or History or Anthropology or anything else to make themselves into a more rounded person, while pursuing an interest in acting, writing, music, DJing, for example, in their spare time.

That's my main advice really. Have a normal life and get a good all-round education while pursuing relevant interests and then try everything you can to get some experience. Even big stations may welcome free help from someone who knows about radio, news and/or music and is willing.

I love my job! It is different every day and involves working with and around people who genuinely love what they do and take real pride in doing a good job and communicating, entertaining and informing as many people as they can.

Any more suggestions?

Mark: I could talk for hours about this and I don't think it's too silly to suggest that people listen carefully to their favourite broadcasters and learn that they need to find a style – their own style. It took me a few years but I find now that I do broadcast as myself. It's also worth practising on HiFis and making home tape recordings, no matter how embarrassing it is, as you need to get used to your own voice and delivery. I also think broadcasters and journalists make very good producers, as they understand what it's like to be in the hot seat.

QUALITIES YOU'LL NEED

So far, what are the qualities you should be able to demonstrate?

You have to be a bold, hard-nosed, **enthusiastic go-getter**. You've donated every spare moment to unpaid work – and been grateful. You eternally demonstrate that **you enjoy a challenge**, you'll have your fingers and toes and everything else crossed for luck to shine down on you and you'll have a foot in every available door and you won't mind the bruising at all.

You've shown a **commitment** to broadcasting, **confidence** to interview anyone from the recently bereaved to the politicians who make your toes curl. Your **effective communication skills** are obvious, as is your ability to see all possible angles of a story. You have enough **personality and vibrancy** to fit in with absolutely any team and your talent for making difficult situations easy deserves medals. You'll also have the qualifications to show that you are the undiscovered brain of Britain and you can make cordon bleu coffee.

More than all of this, you'll have some magical or spiritual ability to be in the fabled 'right place at the right time' and you'll **never give up!**

Wouldn't it be easier to give in to the parents and become a doctor? (The answer is 'yes, but I love radio'!)

Ok, time for a break. Put the book down, log onto the website of the Radio Academy and either download or phone for their CD of 'Getting Into Radio'. It's presented by John Peel and has contributions and advice from all kinds of people in all kinds or areas of radio. (While you're on the site look at the membership details and look into the RA Masterclasses.) Here's the contents list:

- Getting Into Radio – Introduction by John Peel
- Engineering – From studio sessions to digits; an essential guide
- Production – The skills and interests you need to make it
- Sales & Marketing – How to sell yourself into a selling role
- Journalism – Editors and journalists with the inside story
- Commercial production – An insider's guide to 30-second heaven
- Presentation – Presenters on how to get in and get on-air
- Getting into radio – A final thought: never give up!

SUCH HARD WORK! WHAT'S IT ALL FOR?

Neil Gardner is a Creative Director and Senior Producer at Ladbroke Productions (Radio) Ltd, an independent production company. The company was established in 1975 and has produced over 120 programmes for the BBC radio networks including 'Dub It Up with Roni Size' for Radio 1 and 'The True Story of British Pop' for Radio 2. They have their Sony Gold, of course, for 'Ironic Maidens with Susan Jeffries' (look these up!).

Neil's writing has been recognised by two New York Gold Awards (look that up too!). This is what he says about motivation:

There is a certain feeling you get, in the pit of your stomach, when you discover that you've won an award. First you realize that 'yes, I can make a good radio show, I wasn't deluding myself'. Later it dawns on you that by winning a Sony you have also won the respect of your industry peers, as it is those very fellows who choose the winners. It's a great feeling, one of adulation, happiness, joy, vindication for all the years of struggle and toil, smugness, a certain weight off the shoulders and also a tinge of worry ... now I've got to do it again!

However, I would like to make you aware of something that feels even better ... and in many cases is even rarer to receive. I promise you this, the day you get a phone call, email or letter from a single listener who says 'Thanks for making my day', or 'What a great programme', or 'I just wanted to say how much I enjoyed ...', that's the day when you'll be walking on air, flying through the clouds and everything will be all right with the world.

Peer recognition is one thing – we all listen with educated ears to other people's programmes – but to be sought out and recognised and thanked by a listener, who has so much more to worry about, concern themselves with and generally be doing with their lives ... that's when your art and your profession have done their job ... you've entertained someone.

Keep making the shows for those who matter, the listeners rather than the judges. And when you get that right, the Sony Awards will come and find you!

MAKING PROGRAMMES AND THE COMMISSIONING PROCESS

So let's get on with it. This is hard but there is no reason that you shouldn't know about it.

The BBC offers a percentage of its schedule to independent programme makers. Radio 4 will only deal with a list of registered production companies, so you'd have to go through one of those (their website gives a full list). Radio 1's core output is mostly long-running strands so they have 'virtually no commissioning round'. The programmes (mainly 30-minute documentaries) that they do commission are limited to a small number of companies such as All Out Productions and Somethin' Else.

Radio 5 Live makes the same claim but does also commission informally. BBC Radio Scotland and Wales have their own commissioning editors and systems. Radio 2 has official commissioning rounds as well.

In reality, this process is utterly closed to individuals making their pitch to the programme directors of the networks. But if you intend to be the Tarantino of radio (or Merchant Ivory or Spike Lee) there'll be a space for you. This is what the website (www.bbc.co.uk/commissioning/) says:

> The networks produce guidelines for suppliers, which outline the slots available, the kind of programmes being looked for and guide prices. A deadline for proposals is set, after which the networks prepare a short-list and rejections are sent out. After discussions on programme content, delivery dates and the budget, the final list is drawn up.

If you have a potential Sony award-winning idea, the best route could be to take it to an acknowledged radio production company that will then offer it to a network on your behalf. You will need to find what production company ('supplier') to take it to. Don't worry; you'll know who to approach because in your radio diary you'll have noted the ones who have the right relationship with the network you are targeting. You'll have made notes on back announcements, programme credits, names of production companies and the names of the producers.

If you read the trade press such as *Broadcast* or *The RADIO Magazine* (www.theradiomagazine.co.uk/), you'll also find out a lot about which companies are being commissioned on a regular basis. In this way you'll discover the specialities of the production companies. Many of the bigger production companies are well established and have good relationships with all the networks. By the time you make your call with the offer of your programme idea you'll be able to cite their previous programmes and how yours fits in to their style.

Production companies such as Somethin' Else have a track record of working with freelance producers to get ideas commissioned. There are plenty of others all over the country. If you are commissioned you'll be paid to make the programme and you'll receive some of the production fee (the profit) as well. This also means you can get guidance from those used to working with the network, whilst having as much involvement in your idea as your experience will allow.

Here are some pointers for approaching a production company.

You'll have a written script as well as a detailed outline, a first draft of a budget and a list of interviewees that are willing to take part. You will have carried out pre-production interviews to establish the interviewees' involvement and angle, found a willing presenter (you might have been through an agent to get the presenter) and you'll have some awareness of whether the producer guidelines apply to your programme.

As a first step, identify the right person in each production company and approach them with your idea, in one paragraph. If you can't explain the essence of your programme in such a brief space, it's probably too complicated. But even if your contact only wants a little précis, you should have in your back pocket all those other things.

Be familiar with the station you're targeting, its priorities and audience profile. I proposed a programme for Radio 2 at exactly the same time as it was repositioning its appeal in the market and targeting a younger audience. My target age of listener couldn't have been further from the new younger audience it was hoping to attract.

The BBC Commissioning homepage is packed with a bewildering amount of details on the subject, so you really need to know what you're looking for. You could be looking for radio information and find yourself on a page for TV programme production. Nevertheless, take a look around the site if you think a career as a freelance or a career in the independent sector is your goal.

One thing to be aware of is the question of copyright. The copyright in your work is a very important consideration and it's crucial that you assert and protect yours, or make a conscious decision to transfer or sell it. Because it can be very difficult to protect ideas (as opposed to finished work) one way of protecting your copyright is to ensure that your work is clearly marked 'STRICTLY CONFIDENTIAL' when it is submitted.

When you're ready to make your move turn to the *Radio Academy Directory* to find the contact details of the right production company for you.

If you set yourself this task, think of climbing Mount Everest as the easier option. However, it is there to be climbed!

INTERNET RADIO

This is the most exciting thing on the radio scene, especially for people who are starting out. It also goes against a lot of the recommendations in this book about understanding the station you want to work with, knowing the audience profile and staying within those profile boundaries and, for music radio, knowing the playlist and staying within an age range. Forget all of that. This is where you make the rules.

To get advice from the horse's mouth, I went to Mike Chapman who helped to establish SpydaRadio, which is an Internet radio station. It was born in 1999 out of the ashes of CMR (Country Music Radio) and with a couple of people from the old BBC GLR 94.9.

SpydaRadio DJs play to a 'wide audience profile' with no regulated playlist and the shows are archived and available anywhere in the world. They struck a deal with two partner venues (The Borderline in London and The Joiners in Southampton) to promote live music and raise revenue. They also generate income via listener donation. Take a look at the website: www.spydaradio.co.uk.

I asked Mike to tell me everything you need to know about being a lone ranger radio presenter/producer/manager in the privacy of your own home. He's written from the point of view of a music radio producer. For speech radio you'll be playing out packages from your hard drive instead of, or as well as, CDs. You may already have dabbled in playing around with a little studio linked up to a PC. Otherwise, you'll have some homework to do but this is very achievable so read on.

Here's what he advises:

How to get your own radio show onto the Net

You will need a home studio:

- a simple mixing desk, costing about £160.00
- two CD players so that you can mix the tracks
- a good quality microphone, probably £80.00, for your introductions

This 'studio' can plug into the back of the computer, into the **soundcard**, so that you can record your shows directly onto the hard disk.

You will need mixing software, something like **CoolEdit**, which creates a **WAV file**. (The file size will be quite large so you will need a lot of memory in the computer. A three-hour show takes up about 900mb.)

You will then need to convert the WAV file into a **streaming file** through your streaming software. Windows Media is already provided on all PCs and RealAudio can be downloaded for free from the RealAudio site. When the file is converted into a streaming file the size will be reduced quite considerably.

The streaming file has to be uploaded to the site that is going to stream your show, so you will need an **FTP programme**. Smart FTP is available as a free download. It is very easy to operate and very quick.

Finally you need a **host site** that will hold your show in cyberspace, so that your listeners can tune in. For a beginner you will want to use a ready made site that is inexpensive.

The only one that we could find is an American site **live365.com**, which has a variety of packages starting at $7.45 per month to host a show of 100mb in size. As a guide, a three-hour show in **narrowband** is approximately 35mb, in **broadband** it would be approximately 100mb.

The advantage of using a site like live365.com is that it takes care of all the details involved in Internet broadcasting. It can help with marketing, making sure that all royalty issues are dealt with, etc.

So have a go, but keep it simple. If you are producing a music show, let the music predominate, don't get carried away with the sound of your own voice, don't ramble; less is more!

USEFUL SITES
www.realaudio.com
www.live365.com
www.syntrillium.com (for CoolEdit)
www.smartftp.com
www.cakewalk.com (to get an idea of home studio equipment).

'Look at the skills you can offer. You'll be creative and have the ability to deal with a variety of subjects.'

training, CVs, ambition

So, what are 'transferable skills'? Well, they're skills that you can apply in many different jobs and situations – for example IT skills or the ability to communicate well, which are valuable in any work situation. If your first step on the work/work experience ladder is spent in a radio station, look at the skills you can offer to your next employer in a different career choice. Your writing will be clear and concise, you'll be creative and have the ability to deal with a variety of subjects. You'll be a careful researcher and be able to pick out interesting facts. You'll have a second nature of meeting tight deadlines, your time keeping will be marvellous and you'll have technical abilities. You'll be adept at what the media calls 'multi-skilling'.

Some people take their radio skills and move from radio into teaching. Some move into press officer jobs. There are all kinds of researcher jobs out there with universities, government departments and the aid and charity world. Here's the story of a friend of mine who moved from radio into a career as a celebrity agent.

Julia Chapman: Senior manager with NCI Management Ltd

NCI Management Ltd is an agency offering a 'total management service' to around 25 clients. Most are television presenters and specialists of various kinds such as agony aunts, psychologists, broadcasting doctors and DIY presenters. A radio client of hers, Stephen Nolan, recently won two Sony Gold Awards for a programme he presents on Belfast's City Beat – an unprecedented achievement. I asked Julia how her journey through radio brought her to this job.

What skills do you need to be an agent? What does the job involve?

Julia: My job involves finding new talent and then finding that talent work, negotiating their fee, terms and conditions and going over the contracts. Once they are in the job I look after their publicity and corporate work, any book deals and newspaper columns. I make sure they are happy at work and may have to sort out any disputes with producers or fellow presenters. For our PR clients, the company tries to raise awareness about them as much as possible with functions, fundraising events, press and TV and radio appearances.

So, back to your radio beginnings. Where did you start?

Julia: I graduated from Bournemouth University in 1990 with a 2:1 in Communication and Media Production. It is a myth that media courses are not useful. There are good and bad, the same as any other type of course. Everyone I know of from my course is now doing really well in various fields of the media and earning good salaries. It covered practical aspects of TV and radio production and computer graphics (editing, vision and sound mixing, studio and camera work, as well as television and radio analysis and communication processes). We studied media law and wrote a dissertation in our final year, so the course had a strong academic bias as well.

Was it difficult to get on to your course?

Julia: Most people on my course had Oxbridge degrees as it was one of the hardest courses to get on to in the country (even though it was a polytechnic at the time). Many of my peers had four grade As at A-level but some people, like me, managed to shine at interview without having brilliant grades. I had

A-levels in English Literature, Sociology and Geography with average grades and ten O-Levels in Maths, English Lit and various others (you had to have those two, but I can't remember what my others were in).

What was your first job?

Julia: After the course, I worked as a production assistant in BBC local radio, working my way up to being a reporter and researcher very quickly. I gave up my job after about a year and a half and went travelling around the world for six months. When I got back, I got a job as a programme assistant (next rung up), then producer, then senior producer in local and regional BBC radio (I did a bit of TV too, for the elections of 1992). I then left to go to work as a producer for Talk Radio when it launched. It was very exciting to be in at the launch of a totally new concept in speech radio.

It sounds like a charmed career ladder. What happened?

Julia: I loved working in radio but got to the stage where I was not challenged any more and got fed up with the constantly changing staff, management and office politics.

How did you make the move?

Julia: I moved into being an agent by accident. One of my researchers was Mike Sissons (son of Peter Sissons, the newsreader). Peter gave me a lift one day and asked me what I fancied doing work-wise. I said I'd like to be an agent and he said his agents were looking for someone. I started as their assistant (by this time I was about 24) and soon became an agent. I only worked there for a while, before I was headhunted by another agency where I worked for four and a half years before I worked here at NCI.

Transferable skills?

Julia: Loads of contacts. Most of the people I have worked with are useful to me or have become clients. I also learnt in radio how to 'keep lots of balls in the air at the same time', which is useful when you need to know what 25 clients are up to at any one time. I also gained a lot of confidence in being able to cope with anything that's thrown at me and learnt to work to a deadline. Both jobs are all about people skills, which I'm strong on. Learning about contracts and copyright at university was really useful too, but you get better at all that the longer you've been in the job.

TRAINING

What do you think? Do you still think it's for you? People who love radio really do love it! It's an industry that adores people of independent spirit who are hugely capable and creative.

Take a look around you at the courses on offer – a list is given in the final chapter. To help you find the right course you could look at the website for the Broadcast Journalism Training Council, which is an organisation that gives industry-recognised accreditation to courses for radio and TV. The website has links to those courses.

Here are some things to think about when wading through the jungle of courses on offer:

- What do they expect you to gain from the course: what skills, access to facilities, suggestions about moving forward, follow-up support, suggested contacts?
- Who is teaching on the course? Are they working in the industry or not? Find out what practical help they can be.
- Be very specific about your own skills and whether the course will recognise your talents and interests.

There are scare stories about how terrible media courses are. Well, if you do very careful research and are determined about where you want to go in the industry you'll find the right course, short or long.

If you're interested in drama, don't do a news course! It sounds obvious, but I have to admit that when I took a media postgraduate course I couldn't have been more foolish about the choice I made. The course had a magnificent reputation but the content didn't suit me at all. I was motivated by having the qualification from this reputable university on my CV. It was a ridiculous reason. I didn't last very long and it was an expensive mistake.

Have a look at the **IDEAS**FACTORY website's Training & Courses section, to consult an advisor about the best course to do, and search for courses. www.ideasfactory.com/training_courses/index.htm.

I was really impressed with the courses database on Connexions Direct. (www.connexions-direct.com/section.cfm?sectionId=66). I simply put 'radio' into their search engine, didn't fill in the location box or the level box and hit 'search'. All kinds of wonderful courses came up. The part-time evening courses were listed together with the postgraduate ones. Courses that are privately run and cost a fortune are listed alongside the adult education part-time courses that don't cost much at all.

YOUR MAGNIFICENT CV

By now you'll have something to say for yourself. You'll have your work experience tucked safely under your belt and, as a result, a referee. You'll have organised your regular voluntary gig so you'll be able to show evidence of experience, enthusiasm and commitment. You'll have hands-on experience of equipment so you'll be able to write a 'skills' section in your CV. You'll have a crystal-clear idea of your ultimate goal. Aren't you a catch!

There's plenty of help you can get in writing a CV. Many radio stations take into consideration the trouble and concerns of people who want a radio career. They've been incredibly generous in giving information and examples on their websites.

Take a look at what the BBC has to say on its 'One Life' website, www.bbc.co.uk/radio1/onelife/work/index.shtml?cvs#topics. It not only goes through the content but also the appearance and length of your document. Channel 4's **IDEAS**FACTORY website also has a Plan Your CV section with useful advice and hints on creating the best CV possible. Go to www.ideasfactory.com/careers, then click on 'Knowledge', and you will find a CV-making tool.

Just a note about the 'speculative' CV. I spoke to Roger Hammet, a careers adviser at the BBC, who emphasised that they are not welcome. Generally speaking, he said, 99.9 per cent of BBC applications are done on a template provided online in response to advertised vacancies. The small percentage of those who don't use the technology either don't have access to IT or may have a disability that precludes it.

Independents, he said, may have a different policy but the unfocused, unsolicited CV at the BBC will go straight in the bin. So, forget it if you thought you could write one CV and one covering letter and send it to every possible employer. You have to spend much more time than that to present yourself at your best. However, the plus side is that you'll be sending out highly tailored, highly focused letters that are more likely to impress.

Roger Hammet gave me three points that a CV must display. These are the key things:

1. Show your passion for the industry
2. Identify your skills and experience
3. Focus on a particular job in the industry – show that you have a goal and that you're driving towards it.

Check out job adverts in the media section of the *Guardian*. What do they ask for? Get used to the requirements of the type of job you are going for.

What if you're expected to provide a demo tape? I checked with Andy Brown at Radio 1 how he produced his. He said he was advised to produce a mixed package of no more than three minutes. He found a DJ to introduce him then went straight into some of his football commentary. He followed that with a live phone-in and ended with an 'and finally'-type, light piece. He also said that he was advised not to use other male voices in case they sounded too close to his voice or better than his, and anyway the piece needed a male/female mix. Where a male voice appeared in his featured interviews he faded them out for the close.

WHAT IT'S LIKE TO GET A SONY

I was wondering who to ask for their take on a night at the Sony Awards and I came across the website of Fiction Factory. It calls itself 'an association of professional producers and directors' and says that it makes 'products of the imagination'. This is right up my street. They won a gold Sony Drama Award for 'Plum's War' (a drama about PG Wodehouse). I called John Taylor and asked him to describe the evening and his moment of glory. Here it is:

The writer (we'll call him Will) and I arrive at the hotel by the back door because we decide the car we hired from Rusty's Cabs isn't going to look too good swishing in at the main entrance. Besides, this is a black tie do, and Will has forgotten his black tie.

Considering this is radio, they've gone to town with the visuals. The hotel's enormous reception room has a gigantic plasma screen to flash up details of the winners and inject some pizzazz into what is basically going to be an evening of food, booze and speeches. Hundreds of tables crowd around the stage, and all the diners are hoping for a big prize.

The way the Sonys work is this: five nominees in each award category are invited to the ceremony, the first three get gold, silver and bronze awards and the other two go home sobbing. There are a lot of glittering people about and Will and I begin to feel distinctly as if people who come in rusty cabs without black ties probably aren't in with much of a chance. We get our hankies out ready and sit down to eat.

The lighting is pink and violet and makes my plate of Chicken Manhattan look like nuclear fallout. I switch off my Geiger counter and tuck in. Important people begin to speak. The distinguished installation artist Tracey Emin has been invited to talk to us about radio. She declares that she considers it to be very suitable for blind people, a remark which causes someone on our table to respond rather unkindly, 'A bit like her art then'. Will, already bored, and not expecting to win anything this evening, spots Jamie Theakston at another table and goes to get an autograph for his daughter.

Actually Will is a very good radio writer. One of the best. But while they are giving out prizes for the loudest music, the raunchiest talk-show and the filthiest breakfast presenter, Will's finely wrought masterpieces of radio drama begin to seem to belong to another cosmos.

Then suddenly they're reading out the drama prize-winners and ... they must have got it wrong ... they think it's for us. It is for us. 'Will! It's for us!' Will and I embrace – just long enough so no one gets the wrong idea about our artistic relationship – then suddenly I'm on the podium being kissed by a beautiful celebrity (female) and handed a heavy lump of transparent plastic. Next thing I know, I'm making this speech which seems to last approximately eight seconds and excludes all those essential plaudits for my sound people, my commissioning editor, my secretary, my secretary's mother and the priest who baptised me, and then I'm back at the table with a Gold Sony Award and an ecstatic writer. Will and I, so as not to waste good handkerchiefs, sob anyway, just for the hell of it.

Final checklist

What have you done so far?

- ■ Decided where you'd like to work in radio?
- ■ Started a regular work experience gig?
- ■ Found out about courses? Found a training centre?
- ■ Written a CV and covering letter?
- ■ Started reading trade papers and radio reviewers in the press?

What will you do next?

- ■ Send out CVs?
- ■ Train yourself in editing skills?
- ■ Collect your published and broadcast work?
- ■ Put together a demo tape?

9. FURTHER INFORMATION

FURTHER READING

Please borrow before you buy. You don't know yet what will be relevant to you and what will be a waste of money. Also, updated versions come out, in some cases, once a year. The industry, its personalities, owners and technology all move on so fast that you need to be careful what you buy on the subject and check the date of publication. It might be worth waiting for the next edition.

Some consider the annual *Guardian Media Guide* a must and, certainly, it has a huge amount of information and contacts and course details. It can be bought in bookshops and ordered from the *Guardian*. This is not a book dedicated to radio; it covers all media. Borrow first – it's not cheap! The small section devoted to radio in the *Guide* gives a list of useful radio websites, contact details for independent national stations, BBC stations and digital stations. There are also pages of contacts for ethnic press, TV and radio.

A Guide to Commercial Radio Journalism by Linda Gage and revised by Lawrie Douglas and Marie Kinsey is published by Focal Press. This is a training manual and so there is a lot you can teach yourself with the help of this book. It's practical. The writer couldn't have been more highly respected in the industry. Once you have your feet under the table in a regular job or voluntary gig, take a look through this book. Borrow it at first! A new edition is sure to come out soon.

Her advice on writing is extensive and it's worth getting as much of this as possible from different sources. Her advice on getting to know your voice and communication skills rather unhelpfully suggests we think in terms of how we communicate in a pub. But it seems to me that pubs are the place to go to find lazy language. My religion doesn't militate against them but my ears do. Do you really want to turn on the radio to find the inane drivel of pub talk? I really wonder why she wrote that.

Linda Gage writes on how to find a story, how to present it and interview techniques. She tells about different programme formats, journalistic codes of conduct and taste and decency. The fantastic thing about this book is the legal detail and advice on court reporting.

Fi Glover is a presenter on BBC Radio 5 Live who has written a book about travelling around the world to find out about 'truly unique' radio. The book is called *I am an oil tanker: Travels with my radio* and is published by Ebury Press. This is not any kind of training manual but it provides a little window into a whole world of radio that exists beyond these shores. This is really a travelogue and a lot of her details are about taking flights, checking into hotels and mixing with the hoi polloi in her different destinations. But it caught my breath to read about Memories Radio in Colombia (see page 47) and it taught me humility when I read about the troops' radio in Lebanon. The story of ZJB radio in Montserrat shows broadcasting as a public information service in the most crucial of circumstances – a volcano eruption.

Basic Radio Journalism by Paul Chantler and Peter Stewart is another Focal Press publication. It has lively, wagging-finger-type advice on shoddy writing, journalese and jargon. It rages against Americanisms and clichés. This is another textbook for broadcast journalists. Everything you need is here. Time spent with this book will demystify the whole radio process for you, starting with an overview of the industry all the way through to 'specialised' programming. The authors cover all the core skills and address both the BBC and commercial sector. They have a wonderful section on the dreaded job interview. They suggest that an interview expected to last one hour merits eight hours of preparation! They talk you through nerves, body language, 'journalistic' tests and awkward questions.

INDUSTRY PRESS

The *Media Guardian* on Mondays should be at the top of your weekly read, for guidance on what's going on in the industry and also your first port of call for what jobs are out there. You'll find not only a comprehensive list of media jobs but also articles on whatever and whoever is significant in radio, print and TV. You'll find out about the choices of producers, editors, owners and media magnates and read about media responses to significant stories and an investigation into the motivations of key players. It's an essential read for anyone looking to get into the industry. It also has an excellent accompanying website: http://mediaguardian.co.uk/radio.

Broadcast Magazine describes itself as the 'UK's only weekly newspaper for television and radio professionals, *Broadcast* spans all sectors with production, programming, facilities, technology, digital and international news'. Like the *Media Guardian* it's read widely in the workplace. Website: www.broadcastnow.co.uk. You can pick it up from newsagents or subscribe on the Internet.

Ariel is the internal weekly newspaper for BBC staff. You can either subscribe to it (01709 364 721) or you can pick it up for free in any BBC building reception. (If you have any friends or relations who work for the BBC then they can pick you up a copy.) It is very useful for information about what is going on within the BBC, and lists jobs that otherwise you may not see advertised.

WEBSITES

Throughout this book there are addresses of useful and interesting websites you should visit. Here is a reminder:

IDEASFACTORY (www.channel4.com/ideasfactory; www.ideasfactory.com/music_sound/index.htm) is a dynamic initiative from Channel 4 to help young people get into the Creative Industries. It covers Film & Television, Music & Sound, New Media, Art & Design, Writing, and Performing in a lively, realistic, networked way. It combines highly practical on-line resources/activity with live production training events and 'real world' support across the UK.

UK Radio.com (www.ukradio.com/) says that it's the 'Radio Industry's most referenced news source. Aimed at the radio broadcast professional and all those with an interest in the industry, this site is updated daily with news collected from radio stations and production houses all over the country.'

Hospitalradio.co.uk (www.hospitalradio.co.uk/) is an impressive source of news and links – not only links to hospital radio stations but also radio industry links and news, technical information and the offer of some fairly expensive training.

Radio Now (www.radio-now.co.uk/) offers live radio links for UK radio stations and DAB digital radio live online, a directory of national and local stations, radio news from the industry, information on brand new radio stations on digital, AM, FM and on the Internet and features on digital radio.

Media UK (www.mediauk.com/) has been one of my favourite finds in the research for this book. The latest media jobs section gives listings of paid and volunteer jobs (www.mediauk.com/directory/radio/). I found these examples: a Kent-based RSL wanted a drive-time presenter, a Poole RSL wanted staff, a Wolverhampton RSL wanted volunteers and Staffordshire's 'newest radio station' wanted everybody!

Radiofile (www.radiosupport.co.uk/) is a site for information on short-term licences and is 'self-running'. It welcomes you to register in order to post your pictures, news, calendar events and web links into its open database.

TRAINING ORGANISATIONS

Broadcast Journalism Training Council
You can find courses here that 'are accredited or are seeking accreditation from the BJTC. Accreditation means that a course meets the standards set down in the Council's guidelines.'
Tel: 020 7727 9522
Email: secretary@bjtc.org.uk
Web: www.bjtc.org.uk/courses.html

City and Guilds
Look at the course for Media Techniques – Journalism and Radio, levels 2–3. This is not a pure radio course but their search engine will find the closest course provider with its post code search engine.
Tel: 020 7294 2468
Email: enquiry@city-and-guilds.co.uk
Web: www.city-and-guilds.co.uk. Do a search for scheme numbers: 7790 and 7500.

Commercial Radio Companies Association
Look at the 'Working in Radio' section of the website where you'll find information on placements and courses.
Tel: 020 7306 2603
Email: info@crca.co.uk
Web: www.crca.co.uk/workinginradio.htm

Community Media Association
Runs courses in radio production and management, particularly for volunteers working on RSLs. Look at the 'Access Radio' page on the website, which gives news (not training information) on local and community radio.
Tel: 0114 279 5219
Web: www.commedia.org.uk/accessradio/index.htm

CROW – Community Radio Workshop
A voluntary organisation that works in association with community broadcasters in the South East (based in Brighton) and claims to be the premier radio skills training organisation, 'particularly (for) those marginalised by race, gender, age, physical ability, colour, religion and sexual orientation.'
Tel: 01273 420520
Email: crowradio@mistral.co.uk
Web: www3.mistral.co.uk/crowradio/courses.html

CSV Media
Full-time training courses in radio production and journalism for unemployed people and industry practitioners seeking to acquire new digital skills.
Tel: 020 7278 6601
Email: media@csv.org.uk
Web: www.csv.org.uk

Hospital Broadcasting Association

Gives details on local hospital radio stations. This is where you'll find hands-on training. You don't pay any money unless the hospital volunteers' sector has a membership scheme, which won't cost very much at all. All you have to do is commit time.
Tel: 0870 321 6000
Email: info@hbauk.com
Website www.hbauk.com/

Mediafly Academy

The Mediafly Academy provides a nine-evening training course in basic radio skills. It's an introduction to commercial radio with Bristol's Vibe 101, Manchester's Galaxy 102 and Galaxy 105 in Leeds. The course is aimed at 15–24-year olds. It's not cheap but there are *free* places if students are recommended by charities or are suffering hardship.
Web: www.galaxy105.co.uk/radiotraining.asp; click on FAQ and course prices for details.

London Academy of Radio, Film & TV

An institution that tends towards TV and film but has a radio production course and offers public speaking instruction. Aimed at people who are looking for a new career and who want to update their existing skills. Courses are run on a day, evening and weekend basis.
Web: www.media-courses.com/ or www.radio-film-tv.com

The Radio Academy

A great site! Take a look around. Consider joining and taking advantage of the masterclasses.
Email: info@radioacademy.org
Web: www.radioacademy.org/masterclass/index.html

Radio Authority

You can find out about RSLs and Access Radio. Keep checking in to see if an RSL is coming to your area.
Tel: 020 7430 2724
Web: www.radioauthority.org.uk

Radio in London

'Whether you're looking for a postgraduate qualification or a short taster course in radio production – whatever your needs and requirements, you can usually find a training course somewhere in London.'
Web: www.radioinlondon.com/training/radioprod.htm. You can also find RSL information at: www.radioinlondon.com/stationguide/rsls.htm

Virtual Radio University (VRU)

'The Virtual Radio University (VRU) is a free resource for UK radio presenters, journalists, sales people, managers, trainees – in fact *anyone* working in (or aspiring to work in) radio and who wants to understand more about the medium and its history.' It's a very generous site and gives very detailed information.

Web: www.radiouniversity.co.uk/univinfo.htm

Women's Radio Group

Offers basic radio production, drama writing/production. Women's Radio Group is a training and networking charity for women interested in radio. Also offers the WRG Online Directory.

Tel: 020 7241 3729
Fax: 020 8995 5442
Email: wrg@zelo.demon.co.uk